ELIE WIESEL

Elie Wiesel: Humanist Messenger for Peace is part biography and part moral history of the intellectual and spiritual journey of Elie Wiesel, a Holocaust survivor, human rights activist, author, university professor, and Nobel Peace Prize winner.

In this concise text, Alan L. Berger portrays Wiesel's transformation from a pre-Holocaust, deeply God-fearing youth to a survivor of the Shoah who was left with questions for both God and man. An advisor to American presidents of both political parties, his nearly 60 books voiced an activism on behalf of oppressed people everywhere. The book illuminates Wiesel's contributions in the areas of religion, human rights, literature, and Jewish thought to show the impact that he has had on American life. Supported by primary documents about and from Wiesel, the volume gives students a gateway to explore Wiesel's incredible life.

This book will make a great addition to courses on American religious or intellectual thought and those interested in further exploring Wiesel's universe.

Alan L. Berger is the Raddock Family Eminent Scholar Chair for Holocaust Studies at Florida Atlantic University, USA. He has lectured on Jewish religious and cultural thought in America, Europe, Israel, and Japan.

ROUTLEDGE HISTORICAL AMERICANS

SERIES EDITOR: PAUL FINKELMAN

Routledge Historical Americans is a series of short, vibrant biographies that illuminate the lives of Americans who have had an impact on the world. Each book includes a short overview of the person's life and puts that person into historical context through essential primary documents, written both by the subjects and about them. A series website supports the books, containing extra images and documents, links to further research, and where possible, multi-media sources on the subjects. Perfect for including in any course on American History, the books in the Routledge Historical Americans series show the impact everyday people can have on the course of history.

ELIE WIESEL
HUMANIST MESSENGER FOR PEACE

ALAN L. BERGER

Routledge
Taylor & Francis Group

NEW YORK AND LONDON

First published 2021
by Routledge
605 Third Avenue, New York, NY 10158

and by Routledge
2 Park Square, Milton Park, Abingdon, Oxon, OX14 4RN

Routledge is an imprint of the Taylor & Francis Group, an informa business

© 2021 Taylor & Francis

Library of Congress Cataloging-in-Publication Data
Names: Berger, Alan L., 1939– author.
Title: Elie Wiesel : humanist messenger for peace / Alan L. Berger.
Description: New York, NY : Routledge, 2021. | Series: Routledge historical
    Americans | Includes bibliographical references and index.
Identifiers: LCCN 2020053421 (print) | LCCN 2020053422 (ebook) |
    ISBN 9780415738224 (hardback) | ISBN 9780415738231 (paperback) |
    ISBN 9781315817538 (ebook)
Subjects: LCSH: Wiesel, Elie, 1928–2016. | Wiesel, Elie, 1928–2016—Criticism
    and interpretation. | Wiesel, Elie, 1928–2016—Religion. | Jewish authors—
    United States—Biography. | Holocaust survivors—Biography. | Human
    rights workers—United States—Biography. | Jews—United States—Identity. |
    Judaism—United States—History. | American literature—Jewish authors—
    History and criticism.
Classification: LCC PQ2683.I32 Z583 2021 (print) | LCC PQ2683.I32 (ebook) |
    DDC 813/.54 [B]—dc23
LC record available at https://lccn.loc.gov/2020053421
LC ebook record available at https://lccn.loc.gov/2020053422

ISBN: 978-0-415-73822-4 (hbk)
ISBN: 978-0-415-73823-1 (pbk)
ISBN: 978-1-3158175-3-8 (ebk)

Typeset in Minion
by Apex CoVantage, LLC

This volume is dedicated to my grandchildren, Eliana, Jackson, Julian, and Ari. May they prosper in and contribute to the growth of a better world.

CONTENTS

PART II
Documents **141**

ACKNOWLEDGMENTS

I am delighted to acknowledge the following people from whose wisdom I have learned: Judith Ginsberg, Martha Hauptman, Barbara Helfgott Hyett, Carolyn Johnston, Henry Knight, Asher Milbauer, David Patterson, Alan Rosen, and John Roth. Graduate students, both past and present, were conversation partners along the way: Dennis Hall, Dyanne Martin, Jenn Murray, Jason O'Connor, and Lucas Wilson. Victor Menco Haeckermann tirelessly tracked down recalcitrant footnotes. Ms. Bonnie Lander, my assistant, with great patience and abundant skill, prepared the manuscript. Paul Finkelman, Series Editor at Taylor & Francis, is owed a debt of gratitude for his wisdom, insight, and patience. It was also a pleasure to work with Ms. Emily Irvine of the Press. In addition, I thank Ms. Olivia Crvaric and Ms. Merissa Pook of The Elie Wiesel Foundation for Humanity for their assistance in procuring certain images. Many thanks are especially due my wife, Naomi, for her constant support and encouragement.

Timeline

1928	September 30. *Simhat Torah* (rejoicing in the Torah). Elie Wiesel born in Sighet, (Transylvania) Romania.
1944	May, Passover. Wiesel family deported to Auschwitz. Mother and young sister murdered upon arrival. Two older sisters survive.
1945	January. Father perishes in Buchenwald.
1945	April. Wiesel liberated from Buchenwald.
1945	May. Wiesel spends time at Ecouis, France, under the guidance of O.S.E. rescue agency for Jewish orphans. Resumes study of classical Jewish texts.
1946–1948	Wiesel travels to Paris; learns French; and studies literature, philosophy, and psychology at the Sorbonne and the University of Paris. Becomes interested in journalism.
1948	Translates articles from Hebrew to Yiddish for Irgun periodicals, but never joins the right-wing political group.
1949	Travels to Israel for the first time as correspondent for French paper *L'arche*. Becomes Paris correspondent for Israeli paper *Yediot Ahronot*.
1952	Wiesel begins traveling around the world, including to India, as correspondent for *Yediot Ahranot*.
1954	Wiesel has interview with Catholic Nobel Prize winner in Literature François Mauriac, who persuades him to write about his death camp experiences and helps in its publication.
1955	Wiesel, on ship to South America, writes contributing a Prefix almost 900-page book, *un de Velt hot geshvigen, And the World Remained Silent*—containing angry reflections about God and humanity during the Holocaust.

1956	*And the World Remained Silent* is published. Soon after moving to New York as a permanent correspondent for *Yediot Ahronot*, Wiesel is struck and seriously injured by a taxi.
1958	*La Nuit, Night*, in 1960 English translation, is published. Wiesel's memoir has been translated into 30 languages, each of which contains Mauriac's Preface.
1960	*L'aube, Dawn*, Wiesel's first novel, is published.
1961	Wiesel covers trial of Adolph Eichmann in Jerusalem. The Nazi criminal is executed in 1962.
1963	Wiesel becomes American citizen. Publishes *The Town Beyond the Wall (TBW)*.
1964	Wiesel returns to Sighet and visits birth home. Receives Prix de l'Universite de la Langue Francaise for *TBW*.
1965	Wiesel travels to Soviet Union and meets with Russian Jews. He receives National Jewish Book Award for *TBW*.
1966	Wiesel publishes *The Gates of the Forest* and *The Jews of Silence*.
1967	Six Day War. Jewish Theological Seminary bestows honorary doctorate upon Elie Wiesel. This is the first of more than 100 such degrees Wiesel would receive.
1968	Wiesel publishes *Legends of Our Time: Essays and Stories*.
1969	Wiesel marries Marion Erster Rose, also a Holocaust survivor.
1970	Wiesel publishes *A Beggar in Jerusalem*; wins Prix Mèdicis.
1972	The Wiesel's son, Shlomo Elisha, is born. Wiesel serves as Distinguished Professor of Judaic Studies at the City University of New York City (1972–1976).
1972	Publishes *Souls on Fire: Portraits and Legends of Hasidic Masters*. Wins Prix Bordin de L'Academie Francaise.
1974	Wiesel protests against the genocide of Paraguay's Ache tribe.
1975	Wiesel travels to South Africa and condemns apartheid.
1976	Wiesel is appointed the Andrew W. Mellon Professor in the Humanities at Boston University where he is also designated a university professor. He taught at BU until his retirement in 2013.
1978	Wiesel is appointed Chairperson of the President's Commission on the Holocaust by President Jimmy Carter.
1980	Wiesel receives the Prix Liber Inter, the S.Y. Agnon Medal, and the Jabotinsky Award Medal. Says *kaddish* for his father on border of Cambodia while protesting that country's genocide of its own citizens.
1981	Wiesel publishes *The Testament*.

1982	Wiesel appointed the first Henry Luce Visiting Scholar in Humanities and Social Thought at Yale University (1982–1983).
1984	Wiesel goes to jungles in Honduras to meet with Miskito tribe.
1985	Wiesel receives United States Congressional Gold Medal of Achievement from President Ronald Reagan. Speaking truth to power, he urges the president to cancel a planned visit to a German military cemetery.
1985	Wiesel participates in first conference to explore statutes of political asylum or sanctuary for the illegal economic refugees from El Salvador and Guatemala.
1986	December 10. Wiesel wins Nobel Peace Prize. He and Marion speak to Jewish refuseniks in Soviet Union by telephone. Wiesel terms the entire afternoon a "dialogue of human solidarity."
1987	Wiesel and wife Marion establish The Elie Wiesel Foundation for Humanity, which is dedicated to fighting for peace and against indifference, injustice, and intolerance. Wiesel testifies at trial of Nazi war criminal Klaus Barbie.
1988	Wiesel publishes the novel *Twilight*. Wiesel's Foundation sponsors a series of eight international conferences whose purpose is to help "create a world in which atrocities such as the Holocaust, and genocide in Rwanda and Darfur and 'ethnic cleansing' in Bosnia are never forgotten and never repeated." Subsequent conferences were held in Paris, Haifa, Oslo, Moscow, New York, Venice, Tokyo, and Boston.
1990	Wiesel publishes *From the Kingdom of Memory*.
1991	Wesel publishes *Sages and Dreamers, Portraits and Legends from the Bible, the Talmud, and the Hasidic Tradition*.
1992	Wiesel travels to Sarajevo and the Balkans.
1993	Wiesel speaks at dedication of the United States Holocaust Memorial Museum. For the second time he speaks truth to power, urging President Clinton to intervene in the Bosnian situation.
1995	Wiesel publishes *All Rivers Run to the Sea*.
1999	Wiesel publishes *And the Sea Is Never Full* and *King Solomon and His Magic Ring*, a children's book.
2001	Wiesel addresses the Days of Remembrance ceremony in the Capitol Rotunda, Washington, D.C. He is awarded the rank of Grand-Croix in the French Legion of Honor.
2002	Wiesel receives the Star of Romania award from President Iliescu of Romania.

	Wiesel's birthplace home in Sighet is declared The Jewish Culture and Civilization Museum, also known as the Elie Wiesel Memorial House.
	Beit Tzipora Center, named after Wiesel's sister lost in Auschwitz, opens in Kiryat Malachi, Israel.
2004	In July Wiesel delivers speech *On the Atrocities in Sudan* at the Darfur Summit Graduate Center at the City University of New York.
	Wiesel receives the Commander's Cross from the Republic of Hungary.
2005	Birth of Wiesel's grandson, Elijah.
	Boston University founds the Elie Wiesel Center for Judaic Studies. Receives Man of the Year Award from the Tel Aviv Museum of Art, receives the Light of Truth award from the International Campaign for Tibet, and publishes his novel *The Time of the Uprooted*. Wiesel, in concert with King Abdullah II of Jordan, establishes the first Petra, Jordan, Conference, which invited Nobel laureates from many fields and countries to discuss issues that threaten peace. There would subsequently be three additional Petra conferences: 2006, 2007, 2008.
2006	Wiesel's *Night* is chosen for Oprah Winfrey's Book Club. Wiesel and Oprah visit Auschwitz. This is the topic of a special episode of Oprah's show.
2007	A second Beit Tzipora Center is dedicated in Ashkelon, Israel.
	Wiesel attacked by Holocaust denier in San Francisco.
2008	Birth of Wiesel's granddaughter, Shira.
2009	Wiesel accompanies President Obama on visit to Buchenwald.
2010	Wiesel is awarded the National Humanities Medal by President Obama.
2011	Wiesel receives inaugural United States Holocaust Memorial Award for his vital role in establishing and advancing the cause of Holocaust remembrance. The award is subsequently renamed in his honor.
2012	Wiesel publishes *Open Heart*, a type of literary last will and testament, stating his beliefs and hopes for humanity.
2016	July 2. Wiesel dies in Manhattan.
	September 12. House of Representatives unanimously approved resolution honoring Wiesel's life and work.
2017	June 14. Southwest corner of 84th Street and Central Park West renamed "Elie Wiesel Way."

INTRODUCTION

On April 11, 1945, members of America's Third Army liberated Buchenwald, a Nazi concentration camp located near the German town of Weimar. Among the camp's 21,000 emaciated prisoners (news reels would refer to them as the "living dead") was a young 16-year-old boy named Eliezer Wiesel, a native of Sighet, a small Romanian town located in the Carpathian Mountains. Skeletal and traumatized, he had lost his mother Sarah, father Shlomo, young sister Tzipora, maternal grandfather Dodye Feig, and paternal grandmother Nissel in the Shoah (Holocaust). Moreover, his traditional religious world view and belief had been severely challenged. Wiesel himself nearly succumbed to food poisoning after liberation. Recalling the American troops who liberated him, Wiesel wrote, "Like lost children, the American soldiers wept and wept with rage and sadness. And we [prisoners] received their tears as if they were heartrending offerings from a wounded and generous humanity."[1]

This was Wiesel's first encounter with Americans. Ultimately, it led to his becoming a naturalized American citizen and an unofficial advisor to presidents of both political parties. Four decades after liberation (a biblical generation; forty years denotes the time period the Israelites wandered in the desert following their exodus from Egypt), he threw out the first ceremonial pitch in the second game of the 1986 World Series between the New York Mets and the Boston Red Sox. During that 40-year period Wiesel, a resident of New York City, had become a naturalized American citizen, although for several years he had been a stateless person. He always expressed gratitude toward his adopted country: "The day I received American citizenship was a turning point in my life."[2] Elisha, his son, recalls that "every time we'd come back to JFK, his eyes would tear up a little when a customs official would stamp his passport and say welcome home."[3] Following his passing (July 2, 2016), the United States House of Representatives unanimously approved a resolution honoring Elie Wiesel's life and work (September 12, 2016). On June 14, 2017, the southwest corner of 84th Street and Central Park West was renamed "Elie Wiesel Way."

Who was Elie Wiesel? He was a Holocaust survivor, champion of human rights, award-winning author, professor—first at City College of the City University of New York where he was Distinguished Professor of Judaic Studies (1972–1976), and then at Boston University where he was the Andrew W. Mellon Professor in the Humanities and university professor for nearly four decades (1976–2013) and was named an outstanding professor. He was also the first Henry Luce Visiting Scholar in Humanities and Social Thought at Yale University (1982–1983). As if to underscore the synergy between his teaching and writing, Wiesel often said that the teacher in him was a writer and the writer in him was a teacher. As a professor his teachings and thoughts impacted the lives of countless thousands of American and foreign-born students. President Ronald Reagan awarded Wiesel a Congressional Gold Medal, and Queen Elizabeth conferred upon him the title of honorary knight. Wiesel also held the Grand Cross in the French Legion of Honor and received the Order of the Star of Romania.

He was a world figure and Nobel Peace laureate who had an enormous impact on American and global culture. Wiesel's council was sought by both Democratic and Republican presidents. Moreover, he captured the attention of millions with his tales, books (he wrote nearly 60), essays, and public lectures. He had come to personify Holocaust survivors and their insistent message about the centrality of Holocaust memory, especially after 1978 when President Jimmy Carter named him chair of the United States Holocaust Memorial Council, predecessor to the United States Holocaust Memorial Museum. Yet all along Wiesel had been writing and publishing books, passionately advocating for memory, and speaking up about the survivors. In addition, he became an activist on behalf of the world's victims of injustice. Neutrality, he observed, always helps the executioner, never his victim.

Among the many paradoxes that defined his life, Wiesel, who was steeped in Judaism and its sources, had a profound impact on Christian theological speculation. His response to the American "death of God" movement reveals the distinctiveness of his relationship with the deity as well as his differences with those in the Jewish community who advocated for this view, especially Rabbi Professor Richard L. Rubenstein and Professor Michael Berenbaum. Chapter 2 discusses his impact on Christian thinkers and clergy as well as the death of God issue. His multitude of friends included diplomats, statesmen, cultural figures, and scholars. A partial sampling includes Kofi Annan, former head of the United Nations; Ted Koppel, the renowned newsman; the Dalai Lama, leader of the Tibetan community, who, like Wiesel himself, was exiled from his homeland; Golda Meir, Prime Minister of Israel; Rabbi Irving (Yitz) Greenberg, distinguished scholar and interpreter of the American Jewish community; and Oprah Winfrey. He also interacted with various diplomats and statesmen from countries as diverse as France, Israel, and Sweden. Among his teachers in America were two illustrious faculty members at the Jewish Theological Seminary, Abraham Joshua Heschel, Professor of Social Ethics and Mysticism, and the Talmudic scholar Saul Leiberman.

Following the end of the Holocaust, Wiesel spent several years in France learning the language (most of his work appears first in French) and supporting himself in a variety of endeavors including choir director—he had a marvelous singing voice and years later he gave a public concert at the 92nd Street YMHA (Young Men's and Women's Hebrew Association), a venerable cultural institution long noted for its public programs. He also supported himself as a camp counselor, tutor, and translator. In addition to learning French, he became a student at the Sorbonne and the University of Paris studying French literature, philosophy, and psychology. Wiesel also began immersing himself in non-Jewish sources and was influenced by the works of Albert Camus, Fyodor Dostoevski, Andre Malraux, Friedrich Nietzsche, and Jean-Paul Sartre. The Catholic writer François Mauriac, winner of the 1952 Nobel Prize in Literature, encouraged Wiesel to write the volume that became *Night* (*La Nuit*, 1958) and contributed the Foreword. The memoir was originally published in Yiddish as *Un di velt hot geshvign, And the World Remained Silent* (Argentina, 1956). *Night* was the considerably condensed French translation. In the late 1950s and early 1960s Wiesel also became a reporter for *Yediot Ahronot*, an Israeli newspaper. He traveled extensively during this time, especially to Israel—he was there for the Six Day War—went to Russia twice, and learned English while in India. He subsequently moved to New York in 1956 where he covered the United Nations for the Israeli paper. In America he became a naturalized citizen in 1963. He contributed essays on cultural matters and reviews to the venerable Yiddish newspaper *The Daily Forward* (or in Yiddish *Forverts**), which is now published online in English and Yiddish, for which he also worked. Later, he was the co-founder, along with Leonard Fine, of *Moment*, a magazine of Jewish culture. Wiesel married his wife,

---

* *The Daily Forward* is a revered Yiddish newspaper that was a lifeline for Jewish immigrants to the United States, especially Yiddish - speakers from Eastern Europe.

** The YMHA and YWHA (Young Men's and Women's Hebrew Association) was long noted for its commitment to sponsoring cultural events.

the Viennese-born Marion Erster Rose, also a Holocaust survivor, in 1969. Their son, Shlomo Elisha, was born in 1972.

Wiesel's thoughts and writings were the product of multiple influences. First and foremost among them were Jewish cultural and religious traditions and their rich textual sources beginning with the Bible and Talmud. He also was a keen student of Jewish mysticism, especially Hasidism. During his student days he was influenced by French existentialism, particularly the writings of Camus and Malraux. He also had a mysterious mentor named Shushani (Mordechai Rosenbaum). Shushani was a religious virtuoso. He was a survivor who wandered over the European continent and taught Wiesel a great deal about Jewish thought and the nature of God. This influenced the survivor's retelling of Hasidic tales which he first heard as a child from his maternal grandfather, Dodye Feig. Wiesel was also influenced by François Wahl, a cultured and erudite person who taught him French. After Wiesel became an American citizen in 1963, his views were sought on matters of antisemitism, human rights, Israel, bringing Nazis to legal justice, political violence, and genocidal actions. He spoke with the authority of a witness and the moral clarity of one who had experienced the depths of human and theological depravity. The Nobel Committee termed him a "Messenger to Mankind." Wiesel's lectures at the 92nd Street Y in New York City** were important cultural events as were his annual fall public lectures at Boston University and in. Paris, He became a human rights activist and champion of social justice, initially for Soviet Jewry, and then for oppressed people everywhere.

Personally, Wiesel walked a theological tightrope consisting of an endless dialogue between the God-intoxicated youth he had been and the Holocaust survivor that he was. In his Nobel Address delivered in Oslo on December 10, 1986, Wiesel attested that the youth asks, "What have you done with my future? What have you done with your life?" Wiesel responds that he has "tried to keep memory alive" and to fight against forgetfulness. To forget makes us guilty accomplices. "I explain" to the boy "how naïve we were—the world did know and remained silent. And that is why I swore never to be silent whenever and wherever human beings endure suffering and humiliation."[4] His life and his numerous works were a compelling summons to readers and listeners to embrace the eternal quest for peace and social justice. Wiesel followed the well-established Jewish Arguing with God tradition in contending that one could be with God or against the deity, but not without God. Wiesel once told Harry James Cargas that ever since Auschwitz he had been trying to find an occupation for God. Later, I asked Wiesel if he had found one. "Yes," he responded, "but He doesn't listen."[5]

Wiesel's thinking about America was ambivalent and changed over the years. On the one hand, as a Holocaust survivor he recalled and indicted what he perceived as the country's indifference to Jews during the Holocaust. He contended that no one warned us about Auschwitz at a time when world leaders all knew about the death camps. The Jews of Sighet—his birthplace—never had the chance to flee. Wiesel writes in his canonical memoir *Night*, "The ghetto was ruled by illusion that all was well and the Jews had nothing to fear." Specifically, he contends, "Unbelievable but true: The American Jewish community had not responded to the heart-rending cries of their brothers and sisters in Nazified Europe. At the very least, not as they should have."[6] Yet rallies and protests were held, most prominently at Madison Square Garden twice. In 1933 Rabbi Stephen S. Wise, prominent leader of the American Jewish community, led an anti-Nazi rally at the Garden, and a decade later Doctor Chaim Weizmann, the President of the Jewish Agency for Palestine and eventually named Israel's first president, spoke at the same venue.

But the Jewish American community was divided and itself victimized by the very strong current of antisemitism that gripped American culture in the 1930s and '40s. President Franklin D. Roosevelt did far less than he could to intervene on behalf of Europe's doomed Jews. Concerned about being reelected, he had heard the antisemitic comments terming his "New Deal" the "Jew Deal" and did not wish to appear too close to the Jewish community. In 1936 the German American Bund, a pro-Nazi organization, was formed. Its goal was to promote a positive image of Nazi Germany among Americans. Moreover, in 1939 there had been a pro-Nazi rally in Madison Square Garden. Breckenridge Long, Assistant Secretary of State, intentionally obstructed refugee rescue efforts. Wiesel reported that he asked five American presidents why the railroad tracks leading to Auschwitz were never bombed. He received no satisfactory answer.

On the other hand, in the decades following the war and with American recognition of the State of Israel, America had itself changed. Politically, most Americans identified with Israel as a bastion of democracy surrounded by Arab states that were implacable foes led by dictators vowing, in Egyptian President Nasser's chilling words, to throw the Jews into the sea. Many American Jews feared a second Holocaust. Moreover, there was a lessening of the virulent strain of American antisemitism, especially among State Department officials. Long, his obstructionism exposed, was demoted and subsequently retired in 1944. Interfaith activity increased under the umbrella group National Conference of Christians and Jews. Furthermore, the country experienced a renewed interest in Yiddish culture and a commitment to civil rights. Following the creation of the United States Holocaust Memorial Museum, Wiesel spoke warmly about America; the greatness of the country, he contended, lay in its willingness to remember.[7]

Night, a slim memoir of terrifying proportion, was the first of his nearly 60 books. Wiesel often claimed that his memoir began where Anne Frank's diary ended. He termed his memoir both the end of everything and the beginning of everything. What ended was his childhood (child-like) messianic belief in a deity who intervenes in history to save the Jewish people in times of grave danger. What began was Wiesel's life-long search for a credible post-Holocaust role for God. The memoir, having initially been rejected by publishers for being too dark, eventually became a universally recognized text of Holocaust literature read in classrooms throughout the world. Wiesel's literary *oeuvre* includes memoir, fiction, and non-fiction. His novels, essays, plays, and public lectures encompass a variety of topics: the Bible, the Talmud, Hasidism, the Holocaust, Israel, Jewish/Christian relations, Soviet Jewry, the Middle East, and Zionism. Moreover, these works appear in a variety of genres: cantata, dialogues, memoirs, novels, and plays. But no matter the genre, the Holocaust and its world-shattering nature is always present.

Wiesel's work on behalf of humanity was recognized through the many honors he received. In addition to the Nobel Peace Prize, he received, as noted, the United States Congressional Gold Medal, the Presidential Medal of Freedom, the French Legion of Honor's Grand Croix, and an honorary British knighthood. Wiesel was awarded more than 100 honorary doctorate degrees from colleges in America and abroad, the first of which was from the Jewish Theological Seminary in 1967; others include Michigan State University, Dartmouth College, City College of New York, Tel Aviv University, Washington University, The Weizmann Institute, The University of Warsaw, and The University of British Columbia. Among his literary prizes are the Prix Bordin de l'Academie Françoise, Prix Medicis, Prix Livre Inter, Prix Rivarol, and two National Jewish Book Awards. Taken as a whole, Wiesel's books, public lectures, and other presentations were, above all else, witnesses for memory. "If we stop remembering," he attested, "we stop being."[8] He worked tirelessly for the preservation of Holocaust memory and exercised profound moral influence in the post-Holocaust world, and was often referred to as the *maggid* (preacher/storyteller) of Sighet. In 1978 President Jimmy Carter appointed him to chair the Presidential Commission on the Holocaust, subsequently renamed United States Holocaust Memorial Council. This appointment, coupled with his many books, public lectures, and interviews, cemented Wiesel's role as the most well-known Holocaust survivor in America. Wiesel led the council until stepping down in 1986. He was instrumental in helping lead the campaign to build the United States Holocaust Memorial Museum in Washington, D.C., which was dedicated in April 1993.

True to the teachings of the Jewish tradition, which was the cornerstone of his identity, Wiesel spoke truth to power. In biblical times this role was played by prophets vis-à-vis kings. See here especially Jeremiah 38:14FF and II Samuel 2–11 (King James Version). Prophets were in danger of losing their lives because of speaking truth to power.

In 1985, accepting the Presidential Medal of Freedom, he spoke truth to power, admonishing President Ronald Reagan on national television on the eve of the president's trip to Bitburg cemetery, which included graves of the SS (*Schutzstaffel*, a veritable state within a state fanatically loyal to Hitler). "That place, Mr. President," said Wiesel, "is not your place. Your place is with the victims of the SS." Less than a decade later (1993) at the dedication of the United States Holocaust Memorial Museum with a heavy rain pouring down amid a sea of umbrellas, Wiesel again spoke truth to power when urging President Clinton not to stand idly by during the Bosnian crisis.

Professor Maurice Friedman described Wiesel as the "Job of Auschwitz" who

> has become the voice and the protest of those who were exterminated and of those who survived the extermination and who have had to contend for forty years with the blight it has thrown on their lives and that of their wives and children and all of those who stand in close contact with them.[9]

Furthermore, Wiesel witnessed the three defining events of twentieth-century Jewish history: the Holocaust, the birth of the modern Jewish State of Israel, and the struggle to free Soviet Jewry. Influenced by his friendship with Abraham Joshua Heschel, Wiesel became an activist on behalf of Soviet Jewry. His 1966 book *The Jews of Silence: A Personal Report on Soviet Jewry* was the work of a witness who was deeply concerned by the plight of his Jewish brethren in the Soviet Union. In addition, it served as an implicit indictment of Western Jewry for not speaking up, and out, loudly enough about the Soviet regime's oppression of its Jewish citizens. The book helped galvanize action on behalf of the beleaguered Jewish population. Moreover, Wiesel increasingly turned his gaze to the issues of universal human rights and social justice in far-flung places across the globe including Paraguay, Cambodia, South Africa, and elsewhere. His point of departure was the teachings of the Jewish tradition. However, he maintained that the more Jewish he was, the more relevant his message was to humanity. He wished to convert no one. Quite the contrary, his hope was to make each person a more authentic member of whatever tradition they adhered to. In 2009 Wiesel accompanied President Obama to Buchenwald. The president said to Wiesel: "Elie, the last word belongs to you."

As his impact grew, Wiesel became the focus of much criticism, especially in France, where he was accused of being too Judeocentric. Yet many of Wiesel's won prestigious French literary awards and he was a well know and appreciated figure in French culture. Of course, no writer is above criticism. However, this accusation strikes me as analogous to those in America who accused the Reverend Martin Luther King, Jr. of being overly concerned about African Americans. Both Wiesel and King, who shared a Boston University connection as King received his PhD there and Wiesel, as noted, taught at the university for nearly four decades, stressed universal themes which emerged from their particularity. Moreover, the notion of social justice was important to each thinker. So too was the insistence that as they spoke and wrote from their own particularity, they addressed all humanity. In addition, both thinkers lived through momentous upheavals in American culture, including political assassinations, one of which claimed the life of Dr. King.

In America, certain critics accused Wiesel of a variety of literary and Holocaust sins. One critic charged that the scene in *Night* portraying the hanging of three Jews at Auschwitz had been invented. A second termed Wiesel a "professional Holocaust survivor." A third went so far as to charge that Wiesel had changed the focus of his memoir in order not to offend a Christian audience. I discuss these critiques in Chapter 1. Others contended Wiesel was unwaveringly supportive of Israel, a country whose presidency he was twice offered, while overlooking Israel's conflict with the Palestinians. I will return to this issue in Chapter 5. Some thought that his last several novels were more ideological than literary. Wiesel convincingly responded to his critics. But one conclusion is that a certain segment of American culture had grown weary of hearing about the extermination of European Jewry and what this might imply for the American future. Wiesel came in for criticism as well in both France and Israel. One dubious French critic accused Wiesel of "collecting the dividends of Auschwitz" for his own personal gain. In Israel the criticism focused on the fact that Wiesel chose to live in the diaspora rather than to make *alyah* (live in Israel). The ultra-Orthodox community derided Wiesel's post-Holocaust trial of God (*din Torah*), claiming that the Holocaust indicted human beings but not the Jewish God.

Wiesel was a frequent White House visitor. The Nobel Peace laureate was invited by President Bill Clinton and First Lady Hillary Rodham Clinton to deliver the Seventh Millennium Lecture, held in the East Room of the White House. His topic was "The Perils of Indifference: Lessons From a Violent Century." He also spoke with President George W. Bush about the Iraq war, urging the president to term it a *police action*. "I cannot be for war," Wiesel told me in a private conversation. President Barack Obama invited Wiesel to the White House on more than one occasion. These White House visits also impacted Wiesel's academic schedule. The oral examination of a PhD candidate whose examining committee was chaired by Wiesel, and of which I was a member, had to be delayed because Elie had been summoned to the White House. Committee members received calls informing us of the postponement the evening before. The exam was held two days later. The committee members were accompanied to the exam venue by a private detective, a bodyguard hired to protect Wiesel after a Holocaust denier had accosted the Nobel laureate in a San Francisco hotel elevator, intent on kidnapping him.

Wiesel tutored presidents on the Jewish historical experience and its contemporary lessons for America. No matter what a president's political party, Wiesel's message always focused on the importance of memory, the necessity of compassion, and the quest for human rights. Indifference, he attested, always helps the torturer and murderer, never the victim. Wiesel was the inaugural recipient of the United States Holocaust Memorial Museum Award which honors those "internationally prominent individuals whose actions have advanced the Museum's vision of a world where people confront hatred, prevent genocide, and promote human dignity." The award was subsequently renamed the Elie Wiesel Award. Individual winners of this award include Representative John Lewis, German Chancellor Angela Merkel, and the Canadian Lieutenant-General Romeo Dallaire. Wladyslaw Bartoszewski, the Veterans of World War II, and all Holocaust survivors (2018) have been recognized.

Wiesel rose to prominence in an America that was undergoing a vast cultural, political, and religious upheaval. The counterculture of the 1960s had long-lasting influence, as did the unpopular Vietnamese war which compelled a sitting president (Lyndon Johnson) not to seek re-election. The rise of the so-called new religions challenged traditional Christian and Jewish explanations of the meaning and purpose of life and post-mortem existence. Economic uncertainty added to a feeling of societal unrest. Beginning in the mid 1960s, civil rights became a policy matter for the State Department. Domestically, the sexual revolution and the rise of the women's movement added to the cultural upheaval. So, too, did the violence in American cities, both north and south, over the rights of African Americans. The assassinations of President John F. Kennedy, Martin Luther King, Jr., Malcolm X, Medgar Evers, and Attorney General Robert F. Kennedy added to national feelings of instability.

In the '70s Watergate became synonymous with political scandal and governmental corruption. The Watergate scandal consumed the nation's interest and spurred widespread calls for political reform and congressional oversight. Consequently, in 1974 the first presidential resignation in the county's history occurred. Moreover, the sexual revolution of the '70s remained a strong cultural current, as did informality in dress. Politically, the New Right emerged as a strong conservative and Christian voice led by figures such as Jerry Falwell and Pat Robertson. The feminist movement grew in strength, prompting a backlash from antifeminists, notably Phyllis Schlafly opposing the Equal Rights Amendment.

Against this background Wiesel brought a message of hope in spite of despair. He interrogated both God and humanity in the wake of Auschwitz and contended that neither party provided satisfactory responses. Wiesel quarreled with God but never abandoned faith. With God or against God, but never without God, was his credo. Just as after the destruction of the Jerusalem Temple in the year 70 C.E., Judaism had to begin anew, so too following the Shoah the world must chart a new course. Not only man died in Auschwitz, Wiesel contended, but also the image of man had been shattered. Memory of the Holocaust, Wiesel attested, will either condemn or save humanity. Referring to the crucifixion of Jesus and its bitter legacy for Judaism, Wiesel observed, "Because one person died two thousand years ago in Jerusalem, every single Jew everywhere, in every country, in every generation, was involved." Drawing a contemporary parallel, he observed:

> Now the whole world lives on the edge of extinction. We live in the shadow of the bomb [which] has become a kind of divinity. And tomorrow, somewhere, anywhere. . . [someone] may push a button—and all of us will either suffer from it or die from it.[10]

Again, the act of one person whom we do not know will involve our very lives. He taught that in the wake of nuclear arms, he believed that the whole world had existentially become Jewish.[11]

Wiesel's life, teachings, and writings have greatly impacted American culture and religious thought. Moreover, as noted, his influence is stamped by paradox. European-born and educated, and steeped in Jewish religious tradition and language, Wiesel's thought is profoundly important, and not only for American Jews. His theological and human rights emphases have also influenced the best among Christian thinkers, as well as those who are secularists. Although he articulated the uniqueness of the Holocaust, Wiesel was also interested in expressing its universal dimension as in his aphorism: "Not all victims were Jews, but all Jews were victims." Viewers of the *Oprah Winfrey Show* heard Wiesel tell Oprah: "To be free is important. To help others to be free is even more important."[12]

Wiesel's work incorporates, and transcends, Jewish values in a manner which sheds light on fundamental American values such as concern for freedom, an abiding interest in religion, striving for an ethical society, and human rights. He and his wife, Marion, an activist in her own right, established The Elie Wiesel Foundation for Humanity with the aim of working toward a more peaceful world. Among the Foundation's projects is an annual essay contest open to college and university juniors and seniors; it encourages students to reflect on an ethical issue of concern to society. The goal is to encourage the leaders of tomorrow to identify issues of paramount concern to society and to begin to formulate responses to these matters. In addition, the Foundation holds seminars in various locations throughout the world where Nobel laureates are invited to deal with issues such as the single-themed "Anatomy of Hate," and "Building a Better World," which was held in Petra. Sadly, the Elie Wiesel Foundation lost over $15 million, stolen by Bernard Madoff. A little more than one third of the amount was recovered and added to by donations large and small from a variety of individuals, Jewish and non-Jewish, children and adults.

The Madoff scandal illustrated far more than the actions of a sociopathic individual. Wiesel responded by saying that a fitting punishment would be for the criminal to sit in a solitary confinement cell surrounded by a screen containing images of people whom he had swindled. Each face would say: look what you have done. Madoff specialized in victimizing members of his own faith. A play called *Imagining Madoff* was based on imagined encounters between Madoff and his victims, the principal victim being Elie Wiesel. The name of the main victim was later changed after Wiesel threatened legal action.

The Madoff outrage continued well past his 2009 trial and subsequent 150-year prison sentence. Deborah Margolin, author of *Imagining Madoff*, wrote it in a manner designed to compare and contrast the immorality of Madoff, the operator of the largest Ponzi scheme in American history, and Elie Wiesel, who represented the epitome of moral authority.

Wiesel termed the play "obscene" and "defamatory," and he labeled Madoff a "thief, scoundrel, and criminal."

Wiesel as "Messenger to Mankind," with a message of moral clarity and the urgency of peace, appears more important than ever for at least two reasons. First, the Holocaust is increasingly becoming trivialized and denied in the post-memorial era. Witnesses are fewer in number. Forgetting is simpler than remembering. Social media, a source of information for many, is, at best, amoral. More often than not it hosts lies about the Holocaust and promotes vile antisemitism, racism, and hatred of the Other. Second, we are living in a time of international terrorism and the emergence of a paranoid style in politics. Two decades into the twenty-first century, a time inaugurated by the international terrorist attack on the World Trade Center and the Pentagon, when extremism in politics and fundamentalism in religion are in the ascendancy, the time is ripe for moral leadership. Moreover, the rancor which many in America display toward their fellow citizens is alarming. Assaults against the truth continue unabated in the era of so-called fake news. Government at the highest level implicitly endorses white supremacy and attacks institutions fundamental to a democratic society. These are deeply troubling signs. As President Abraham Lincoln, then an Illinois senatorial candidate, observed over 160 years ago, "A house divided against itself, cannot stand."

Wiesel's emphasis on questions is a sorely needed balm for our chaotic times. Embedded in the word "question" is the word "quest." This indicates that there is an ongoing search for deeper levels of meaning and for addressing common human problems and aspirations. This stands in stark contrast to fundamentalism and extremism whose adherents have all the answers and therefore see no reason to either speak with or learn more about the Other and themselves. Answers are what extremists provide most often to the detriment of civil speech and amity among people and nations. Extremists offer "certainty" through answers that are unambiguous and dogmatic and that Elie Wiesel never offered specific "answers" but only more questions. While extremists offer dogma and "truth" Elie Wiesel offers nuance as he sought to get people with different view points to listen to each other. "Keeping the dialogical doors open" is preferable to stifling the voice of the Other. Wiesel advocated questions rather than answers. He sought to bring together people of different viewpoints in order to dialogue about their differences. Moreover, there is more than an element of transcendence in the word "question." Its Hebrew rendering, she'elah, contains the name of God—El. This meant for Wiesel that to question means to invoke the deity, to embrace humility, and to respect the Other.

Furthermore, Wiesel's signature phrase, "and yet," is a defiant response to chaos. It keeps open the doors of hope in spite of what might otherwise appear hopeless. "And yet" addresses common human fears and aspirations. In contrast to the limitations of binary logic, "and yet" offers deeper understanding while simultaneously advocating for a better, more hopeful world. It urges us not to be solely reliant on answers, but to keep on inquiring, keep reaching, keep seeking. But this is not a blind faith. Quite to the contrary, it is the type of faith advocated by Rabbi Nachman of Brazlav, grandson of Hasidim's Ba'al Shem Tov founder (the Besht died in 1760), who contended that there is nothing so whole as a broken heart. It is, in other words, only possible to hope and have faith when the worst is known.

NOTES

1. Elie Wiesel, "The America I Love," www.thehypertexts.com/Essays Articles ReviewsProse/Elie_Wiesel_The_America_I_Love.htm. Accessed September 10, 2016.
2. Jeff Jacoby, "Elie Wiesel's Love of America," *Boston Globe*, July 4, 2016.

3. Cited by John Roth, "The Impact of Elie Wiesel," in *Elie Wiesel: Teacher, Mentor, and Friend.* Edited by Aland L. Berger. Eugene, OR: Cascade Books, 2018, page 36.

4. Elie Wiesel, "Nobel Address," in *From the Kingdom of Memory: Reminiscences.* New York: Summit Books, 1990, page 233.

5. Wiesel to Alan L. Berger, September 10, 2009.

6. Elie Wiesel, "Foreword," in *Were We Our Brother's Keepers? The Public Response of American Jews to the Holocaust 1939–1944.* Contributed by Haskel Lookstein. New York: Hartmore House Publishing, 1985, page vi.

7. Wiesel to Alan L. Berger, October 12, 2010.

8. Irving Abrahamson (editor), *Against Silence: The Voice and Vision of Elie Wiesel.* New York: Holocaust Library, 1985, volume I, page 368.

9. Maurice Friedman, *Abraham Joshua Heschel and Elie Wiesel: You Are My Witnesses.* New York: Farrar, Straus, Giroux, 1987, pages 162–163.

10. Abrahamson, *Against Silence*, page 368.

11. Ibid., page 255.

12. John Roth, "Wiesel and Talk About Religion in Public," in *Celebrating Elie Wiesel: Stories, Essay, Reflection.* Edited by Alan Rosen. Notre Dame, IN: University of Notre Dame Press, 1998, page 145.

PART **I**

ELIE WIESEL

CHAPTER 1

SHATTERING THE SACRED CANOPY

Judaism was birthed in the notion of a covenant which, broadly speaking, is an agreement between two parties of vastly unequal power, in this case God and the Jewish people. In general terms, the mission of the Jews, as a chosen people, was to bear witness to monotheism or the oneness of God. The deity, in turn, was to intervene to protect His chosen people in times of great historical danger. Elie Wiesel, like Sighet's other 10,500 Jews on the eve of World War II, was raised to believe in this mythic covenantal framework, which provided a sacred canopy for its adherents. In the words of sociologist of religion Peter Berger, "Religion is the 'sacred canopy' which every human society builds over its world to give it meaning."[1] Living under this canopy meant living under a protective shield which the Jews believed safeguarded them. Symbolically, this canopy is a "shield against terror." It yields order and meaning for believers. Life outside this canopy, however, leads to existential, physical, psychological, and theological chaos. The sacred canopy is what sociologists of religion call a *plausibility structure* that grants purpose to an adherent's life and a transcendent meaning to their death.

Elie Wiesel's story is that of a witness trapped in the kingdom of night. The foundational tenants of his pre-Holocaust Jewish world were radically challenged, Judaism's sacred canopy mercilessly shredded by the Holocaust. In Berger's words, "when the plausibility structure is destroyed, the reality of the world based on it begins to disintegrate (rapidly)."[2] Applying this to Wiesel's situation, it is clear that two antithetical universes confronted one another. Judaism's plausibility structure admonished its adherents to choose life (Deuteronomy 30:19). In stark contrast, Nazism dedicated itself to the death world; murder and the Lord of Death supplanted the sanctity of human life and divine revelation. Mythically, the issue became one of two revelations, the giving of the Torah at Mount Sinai, which yielded a moral and ethical order or *nomos*, and the Holocaust, which Wiesel termed the anti-Sinai, or a world of *anomie*. The tension between the believing youth he had been and the survivor he became marked his post-Holocaust life and work as both a writer and activist on behalf of the oppressed. His experience became paradigmatic for that of Europe's Jews during World War II. Furthermore, Wiesel was a tireless advocate for the importance of Holocaust memory and the multifaceted questions it generates. His influence on American Judaism and the Western world was enormous. Professor Maurice Friedman accurately describes Wiesel's role in American culture:

> For most people, Job is associated with suffering, patience and piety. For Wiesel—Job is associated with trust *and* contending, with wrestling with *God* within the dialogue with God.[3] Furthermore, this ambivalence toward the deity's role in history resonated with the American, non-orthodox temperament.

This chapter places Wiesel in context of his Jewish identity both prior to the Holocaust, during the Shoah, and following his arrival in America. Consequently, several themes are addressed: Wiesel's pre-war God-intoxication and how his image of God was radically assaulted by his Auschwitz and Buchenwald experience; his immersion in Hasidism, which guided everything that he believed; the normative Jewish Arguing with God tradition; his utilization of the *din Torah* (interrogation of God); and his paradoxical "death of God" position in comparison with other major Jewish-American thinkers such as Richard L. Rubenstein and Michael Berenbaum. I distinguished the chapter distinguishes Wiesel's death of God position from that of other Jewish thinkers and discuss his understanding of post-Shoah faith.

WIESEL'S PRE-HOLOCAUST JEWISH IDENTITY

Wiesel from an early age exhibited the traits of a *homo religious*, a religiously committed individual thoroughly immersed in the teachings of Judaism's sacred texts who fervently believed in the coming of the Messiah. For the teenaged Wiesel and two of his close friends, this meant engaging in rigorous ascetic practices, including recitation of incantations prescribed by practical kabbalah (devotional mysticism) under the guidance of their teacher, Moishe the Beadle. Such practices, intended to hasten the Messiah's arrival, had disastrous results for two of Wiesel's companions; Yiddele, the eldest of the three, was rendered mute, while Sruli was also afflicted by physical disability. Wiesel persisted until being deported to Auschwitz. Parenthetically, I note that years later Wiesel traveled to India in the early 1950s. While there he studied Hindu sacred texts such as the Vedas. He also made the acquaintance of a Hindu man to whom he explained Jewish teachings. This man owned a domestic airline that offered free meals on its flights. Wiesel availed himself of this opportunity. More significantly, he rejected asceticism and its attendant suffering. He could stand his own pain, but he could not endorse the pain and suffering of others in the face of so much indifference on the part of so many on the sub-continent.

WIESEL'S BIOGRAPHY

Eliezer (Elie) Wiesel was born on September 30, 1928, in Sighetu Marma-tiei, Romania, a small town in the Carpathian Mountains of Transylvania not far from the Ukrainian border. His birth date corresponds to the Jew-ish holiday *Simhat Torah* (rejoicing in the Torah), a day celebrating the end of the year's public reading of the Torah and the beginning of a new cycle. Wiesel was the third of four children, and the only son, born to Shlomo Wiesel and Sarah Feig. His two older sisters, Beatrice and Hilda, survived the Holocaust. His parents and younger sister, Tzipora, did not. In addi-tion to his parents and siblings, Wiesel's paternal grandmother, Nisel, lived very close to the Wiesel home. Two aunts also resided in Sighet.

From an early age Wiesel was deeply observant. "By day," he writes, "I studied Talmud and by night," he confides, "I would run to the syna-gogue to weep over the destruction of the Temple."[4] He became a disci-ple of Moishe the Beadle, a mystic who aided the 13-year-old youth in his study of kabbalah, especially as it was advanced by the sixteenth-century kabbalist Rabbi Isaac Luria (known as the ARI, Ashkenazic Rabbi Isaac).

Shlomo Wiesel owned a grocery store, many of whose patrons were Christian. He frequently interceded with the authorities on behalf of the Jewish community, and at one point he was jailed for his activities. Although very far from wealthy, he made certain to invite beggars to Fri-day night dinner, and to tell Maria, the family's trusted Christian servant who spoke flawless Yiddish, to prepare a weekly pot of soup for those less fortunate. Shlomo was an emancipated Jew who liked cantorial music and insisted his son learn secular subjects such as astronomy and Hebrew lit-erature in addition to his Jewish religious studies. Although he helped the boy with his study of Talmud and granted him permission to study Jewish mysticism, he insisted that his son learn modern Hebrew. In volume one of his memoirs, Wiesel recalled seeing his father only rarely, except on Shab-bat (Saturday), when they walked together to services. Later, in the death camps, their relationship deepened and they helped one another survive for a time. His father perished in Buchenwald. In *Night* there are only very few pages after the death of his father. Wiesel writes in his memoir:

> No prayers were said over his tomb. No candle lit in his memory. His last word had been my name. He had called out to me and I had not answered. I did not weep . . . but I was out of tears.[5]

Sarah Feig Wiesel was a woman of great culture, a follower of the Wizhnitz Rebbe (Rabbi Israel Hager, born 1860); she also read German literary works. Her dream was that Elie would become a rabbi and a PhD. He became neither. To the degree that a rabbi is both a teacher and a spiritual leader, it is possible to view Wiesel as an unofficial rabbi to much of the world. Sarah was a fervent believer in the coming of the Messiah, which she eagerly awaited. No harm would come to Elie, she believed, because the Messiah would protect him. A very different future was foreseen when Elie was eight years old. Sarah took him with her on her customary visit to the Wizhnitz Rebbe, seeking his blessing for the family. After directing Sarah to leave the room, the Rebbe asked Elie questions about his studies. Next, the holy man dismissed the youngster and beckoned Sarah to return. When she subsequently emerged, she was sobbing uncontrollably. She did not respond to her young son, who wanted to know why she was crying. Twenty-five years later in America, a hospitalized relative who had asked for Wiesel's blessing told him that the Rebbe had said: "Sarah, know that your son will become a *gadol b'Israel*, a great man in Israel, but neither you nor I will live to see the day. That's why I am telling you now."

Sighet assumed near mythic proportion in Wiesel's career as a writer; he kept a picture of his birth home on the wall by his writing desk. The town itself, after the war when Wiesel had become a naturalized American citizen, continued to symbolize his sacred canopy and the world which was swallowed up by evil. Suffused by an atmosphere of messianic waiting, Sighet's Jews were both insulated and isolated from their non-Jewish environment. It was this world which the Holocaust destroyed.

After he became an American citizen, Wiesel visited Sighet on several occasions; the first time in a novel, *The Town Beyond the Wall* (English translation 1964) which, in his words, describes the return "before it actually took place." As an aside, this further illustrates Wiesel's contention that, unlike most writers, his life is a commentary on his work. That same year witnessed his actual return. The first place he visited was the cemetery containing his paternal grandfather's grave. But his childhood Sighet had vanished. Christians lived in all the homes formerly occupied by Jews. Symbols of Christianity, especially the cross, now hung on the walls of their houses. Wiesel visited Sighet on several occasions during the 1990s and early 2000s.

Two other Sighet events deserve attention. In 1964, the date of his first actual visit, Wiesel dug up the watch he had received as a Bar Mitzvah present. He had buried it in the backyard garden before the family was deported in May 1944. He reburied the time piece in the garden. Wiesel, by now a naturalized American citizen, also found one of the few remaining open synagogues in Sighet. It had hundreds of books, including a few that had belonged to him, along with some biblical commentary he had written at age 13 or 14 which revealed his early immersion in Jewish texts and the beginnings of his subsequent emergence as a religious believer. He brought several of these books and commentaries back to America. The synagogue was under the direction of communist minders, although nominally directed by Moshe, (not the pre-Shoah Beadle) one of the few remaining Sighet Jews. But it should be remembered that he was carefully monitored by the communist regime and had no autonomy. Several years later Wiesel again returned to his natal home with an NBC television crew. He again with met with Moshe. Their interview was monitored by communist minder agents whose presence stifled Moshe's response to the question he and Wiesel had rehearsed, i.e., the pressing need for a new synagogue roof.[6] Wiesel's boyhood home was declared a protected historical monument and a museum in 2002. In 2018, after his death, the house was defaced by antisemitic graffiti. The rise of post-Holocaust fascism and antisemitism in Eastern and Western Europe is a matter of great political concern, as it is in America. Not only have Jews been murdered in Europe and the United States, but social media has a penchant for allowing antisemitic and racist hate speech on its websites.

Wiesel refers to Sighet in Edenic terms. It was there that the fervently religious, God-intoxicated youth studied both classical Jewish texts such as the Hebrew Bible and its Talmudic commentaries and interpretations (mishnah and gemorrah) as well as Jewish mysticism. As noted earlier, the youth was especially fascinated by the cosmology of the sixteenth-century mystic Isaac Luria, and the eighteenth-century mystical revival movement known as Hasidism founded by Israel ben Eliezer (BeSHT—Master of the Good Name). As mentioned, Moishe the Beadle was Wiesel's tutor in kabbalah. The young boy learned Hasidism through various tales about the founder. Initially, Wiesel heard these tales and others from Dodye Feig, his maternal grandfather, who lived in the small village of Bitskev, about four miles from Sighet. Wiesel writes of Dodye Feig:

> The stories I most like to tell I heard from my grandfather. I owe him my love of tradition, my passion for the Jewish people and its unfortunate children. And he, who never read a novel, is a presence in my novels. My old men often bear his features sing the way he did, and, like him, disarm melancholy with the magic of words.[7]

His grandfather was a follower of the Wizhnitz school of Hasidism and embodied the spirit of the movement. Elie identified with this school throughout his life.

Wiesel believed that the essence of Judaism is mystical as opposed to rational. The Jews' refusal to disappear from a world that would be more comfortable without them was, for Wiesel, at the heart of the mystery of Jewish persistence. This view led Wiesel to contend that the Holocaust is explicable neither with nor without God. The animating question of Wiesel's life and work from his classical memoir *Night* to his last published work *Open Heart* was: "And God in all that?" Rejecting traditional explanations for the suffering inflicted on the Jewish people, e.g., the biblical notion of exile from the promised land as "punishment for sin" (*mipenei hataeinu*) or the more philosophical idea of suffering as a "reproof of love" (*yessurin shel ahavah*), Wiesel's novels instead implicitly embraced what Isaac Luria termed "the breaking of the vessels" (*Shevirat ha-kelim*), which advanced the notion that a cosmic "flaw" enabled the shattering of vessels designed to contain divine sparks. For Wiesel the Holocaust symbolized the shattering of the vessels.

These sparks were subsequently scattered; some returned to their divine source while others fell to earth. The Jewish people are tasked with raising these sparks (*aliyoth ha-nitsosoth*) by performing every action ranging from eating, praying, sex, etc. with the proper intention (*kavvanah*) of re-uniting God and the *Shekinah* (feminine dimension of the deity). When that is accomplished, the Messiah will appear. Moreover, since the divine sparks have been scattered all over the world, so too have the Jews been exiled in order to raise these sparks. Subsequently, Lurianic thought viewed exile as a mission. Moreover, it is *human actions*, rather than the Messiah, which bring about a "repair" (*tikkun*) of the world. Consequently, the Messiah appears only *after* the world has been restored. Wiesel contended that the Holocaust reveals that "something happened to the relations between man and God, man and man, man and himself."[8]

CENTRALITY OF HASIDISM*

Wiesel's religious identity was intimately formed by his immersion in Hasidism. The Hasidic movement was essentially an eighteenth-century Jewish mystical revival movement which viewed the world as a place of divine enchantment suffused with magic, mystery, and miracle. Eighteenth

---

* Hasidism actually had two beginnings. The first one in the twelfth century was esoteric and involved circulating manuscripts among those whom today we would call theologians. This should not be confused with the eighteenth-century popular movement.

century Hasidism, especially at its inception, can be understood as an attempt to democratize the cosmological teachings of Isaac Luria. Tales, easily accessible to the uneducated, expressed the Lurianic philosophy in a non-cerebral manner; fervor in religious thought supplanted intellectual explanation. Religious enthusiasm took the place of both a dry and rigid Talmud study as well as a rabbinic Judaism, which was susceptible to corruption. A rich oral tradition emerged from Beshtian Hasidism, which provided its followers, the Hasidim, hope. The Besht himself was a charismatic figure who combined the roles of healer, magician, and mystic. Interpreting the Hebrew Bible literally, he taught that God could be found everywhere and potentially in every person. The Hasidic movement encouraged its followers to embrace joy and to reject despair.

Hasidism's world view focused on four elements: divine immanence, worshipping in the material world (*avodah be-gashmiyut*), which blurred the line between sacred and profane, a mystical state of cleaving (*devekut*), which embraced the notion of cleaving to God whose presence is in all being, and the central role it ascribed to the zaddik "just" man or in this case mystic or rebbe.[9] In all of these dimensions Hasidism remained distinct from both rabbinic Judaism and Talmudic study and its secular opponents (*mitnaggdim*). In Hasidism's founding generation, exuberance in worship included practices such as turning somersaults while praying, worshipping when the spirit moved one to do so instead of at prescribed times, and smoking a pipe whose tobacco may or may not have contained hallucinogens. Many of the most extreme features had diminished or disappeared by the time of the third generation, personified by the leadership of Shneur Zalman of Lyadi (1747–1812), author of the authoritative *Tanya*, which articulated the movement's philosophy.

Hasidic teachings were spread not by learned discourse but rather by tales. At its inception the movement was a decidedly oral tradition. Tales enjoyed a two-fold advantage over intellectual discourse or a learned essay. In the first place, they were accessible to all. The unlettered could listen and learn. Second, tales are open-ended. One can raise and re-raise questions, each iteration delving deeper into the heart of the inquiry. The questioning was in fact more important or at least as important as the answer. As noted, embedded in the word question is the word quest, a never-ending and always beckoning command. In addition, we have also noted that the Hebrew word for question *she'elah* contains "El," one of the names for God. Tales were a natural vehicle for social contact and fervor in the manner of Emile Durkheim's "Collective Effervescence." Wiesel was an inexhaustible fountain of Hasidic tales, the telling of which fascinated Americans, both Jewish and Christian, secularist and religious. His lecture series on Hasidism at New York's 92nd Street Y, which eventuated in the publication of several volumes dealing with the Hasidic world, attracted standing room only audiences mesmerized both by the tales and their teller. Other venues for his lectures included Boston University, where he gave an annual series of three public lectures every fall, Paris, and the American *Eternal Light* radio program. In re-imagining the lost world of Hasidism, Wiesel became the pied piper for a life of fervor and spiritual enthusiasm for an America that had achieved great technological advancement but placed far less emphasis on the value of friendship and social connection. Wiesel told a meeting of my seminar at Florida Atlantic University that there were three reasons he returned to Hasidism. First, he said, the Hasidic world "reminds me of my childhood." Second, the movement's stress on simplicity remained compelling. Finally, Hasidism's stress on joy was powerfully uplifting. A handshake, said Wiesel, was a reminder of the Hasidic ethos.[10]

In the post-Holocaust world, many of the European Hasidic dynasties that were obliterated by the Nazis re-established themselves both in America and in Israel.[11] This was accomplished through marriage, by acclimation, or by a distant family relative assuming leadership. Wiesel's nostalgia for and continuing admiration of Hasidism points to the pre-Shoah Hasidic ethos. It was this universe that powerfully shaped his Jewish world view and embrace of the Jewish tradition. Joy and hope, fervor and passion, anchored this universe, along with complete faith in the mystical authority of the Zaddik.

Despite being outwardly exuberant and optimistic, however, there were certain Hasidic leaders who had theological doubts. Zaddikim (plural of zaddik) such as Pinhas of Koretz (died 1791), Barukh of Medzebozh (died 1810), the Holy Seer of Lublin Yaakov YizHak Halevi Horowitz (died 1875), and Naphtali of Ropshitz (died 1827) all, for various reasons, had their own faith issues concerning the delayed arrival of the Messiah and God's evident ambivalence about the Jewish historical experience. In this sense they resemble Mother Teresa (Saint Teresa of Calcutta), the late twentieth-century Roman Catholic saint and Nobel Peace Prize recipient, who, apart from her conservative social positions on matters such as abortion and birth control, expressed her own crisis of faith. Moreover, Rebbe Nachman of Bratzlav, great-grandson of the Besht, aphoristically stated, "There is nothing so whole as a broken heart." Faith is the response to doubt. Despite their theological pain, these zaddikim remained *within* the faith. Wiesel himself, responding to questions from Ariel Burger, his teaching assistant at Boston University, observed the intimate relationship between faith and doubt. "Doubt," he replied, "together with faith, that is good. It can deepen faith and make it more real. Doubt is a kind of inoculation against [believing] we "have more faith than we actually do."[12]

Wiesel's advocacy of Neo-Hasidism, which emerged from his re-reading of Hasidic tales in the light of Shoah and based on his own experience in the death camps, and what he saw as Neo-Hasidism's contemporary message for America and the world, is discussed in Chapter 4 of this volume. For the moment it is sufficient to emphasize the following three elements: fervor, passion, and compassion.

What is, after all, the essence of Hasidism? Wiesel responds to this query by telling a tale attributed to the Besht:

> Do you want to know what Hasidism is?
> Do you know the story of the ironmonger who
> Wanted to become independent? He bought
> An anvil, a hammer and bellows and went to
> Work. Nothing happened—the forge remained
> Inert. Then an old ironmonger, whose advice
> He sought, told him: "You have everything you
> Need except the spark." That is what Hasidism
> Is: the spark.[13]

It is, in short, impossible to be a theoretical Hasid. One must live the life; *experience, not scholarship* or learned discourse, mattered. Another tale: Menachem Mendel of Kotsk, the Kotsker Rebbe (died 1859), heard a disciple complain about the imperfections in creation. The Kotsker replied: "Could you do better? If so, what are you waiting for? Start working!"[14]

Wiesel saw in Hasidism an attempt to ease humanity's existential loneliness. Feeling alienated and isolated, followers of the Hasidic movement were taught that "the road to God leads through man." This assertion is not some elevation of a humanistic impulse. Rather, as Wiesel noted, "everything becomes possible by the mere presence of someone who knows how to listen, to love and to give of himself." Wiesel noted that for him the essence of a Hasidic legend is "an attempt to humanize fate."[15] Joy can displace despair. Friendship is the glue holding humanity together, keeping the absence of hope at bay.

All of this is highly relevant for twenty-first century America, a fractured country with incompetent leadership, mounting racial problems, a dearth of social justice advocates, and confronting a pandemic. Although written nearly half a century ago, Wiesel's *Souls on Fire: Portraits and Legends of Hasidic Masters* inquires why there is a renewal of interest in Hasidic tales. He prefers two basic reasons: post-modern man is "moved and troubled by their message, its loss irrevocably linked to his own inability to believe and persevere." Never "has modern man been more closed to prayer." Perhaps most significant is the fact that all conditions that existed in the eighteenth century are again with us: "physical and emotional insecurity, fallen idols and the scourge of violence." Wiesel saw lessons both spiritual and practical for the American present from the response of eighteenth-century Hasidism to its frequently hostile environment.[16]

Sighet's Jewish population, while interacting with their Christian neighbors principally in business dealings, was religiously isolated and insulated from the town's Christians. Judaism's religious rites and culture meant several things. First and foremost, they visibly signaled that Jews were not Christians. This meant that antisemitic attitudes and actions were a "normal" occurrence. Jesus was venerated by Christians, but in Wiesel's words, "as an adolescent it was a time when between the Christian world and my own there existed only ties of violence and exclusion."[17] Wiesel recalled that as a child he would "cross the street to avoid churches." The second implication is that the very rites and rituals that served to bond the Jewish community marked the community as foreign and *Other*, beyond salvation. Third, the relationship between Judaism and Christianity at that time exemplified what Professor Richard Rubenstein terms "dis-confirming otherness"; for one tradition to be true, the other had to be false. This is a principal reason that the church fervently sought Jewish converts to prove its message superior. To a large extent, this enmity was also the situation in America during the Second World War. Individual Christians and Jews could be friends, but the idea that Jews, as Jews, could be saved theologically was anathema to the Christian world.

AMERICAN ANTISEMITISM

While Wiesel was enduring the abominations of the Holocaust, the attention of most Americans was focused elsewhere. American Judeophobia was freely expressed on both the governmental and individual levels before and even during the Second World War. America retreated into isolation; xenophobia combined with nativism to yield a distinct distrust and dislike of immigrants and foreigners. One need only recall the internment of all Japanese Americans in detention camps. Moreover, the one detention camp for Jews was established only in 1944 in Oswego, New York, a city of very cold winters. The majority of the camp's 980 prisoners came from Italy, a warm weather country. Professor Miriam Sanua Dalin suggests three contributing factors for this mood: the Great Depression inaugurated by the 1929 crash of the stock market, the feeling that World War I had been a colossal failure, and the failure of the peace treaties to bring about stability.[18] Collectively, these factors reinforced the mood of isolation and the America First movement.

The three leading contemporary antisemitic voices in America—Charles A. Lindberg, Father Charles Coughlin, and Henry Ford—normalized

Judeophobia. Lindberg, "Lucky Lindy," the famed aviator, was a well-known isolationist who blamed the Jews for involving America in World War II. Coughlin, the notorious Canadian-American radio priest, was a staunch isolationist and antisemite. A political populist, he broadcast his antisemitic hate speech for many years on the radio. Henry Ford published installments of the notorious 1903 fabrication *The Protocols of the Elders of Zion*, published in Russia, which invented the notion that Jews were trying to take over the world, in the suburban Detroit newspaper *The Dearborn Independent*. *The Protocols* was a volume concocted by Tsarist secret agents at the beginning of the twentieth century and widely disseminated. Its controversial nature made it a best seller. Moreover, President Roosevelt's "New Deal" had begun to be pilloried as the "Jew Deal." Professor Jonathan Sarna reports that

> in 1943 an official government study found substantial amounts of Judeophobia in half of the forty-two states it surveyed, and as late as 1944 fully 60% of Americans claimed to have heard "criticism or talk against the Jews" in the previous six months.[19]

Additionally, antisemitic attitudes were prevalent among high officials of the American State Department. Breckenridge Long, Assistant Secretary of State for Refugee Affairs from 1940–1944, was in charge of the Visa Division whose work directly impacted the lives and fate of refugees. The number of Jews admitted to America during Long's tenure was severely restricted. Long, an admirer of Benito Mussolini, when called to testify before congressional investigative bodies about the situation of refugees, adopted two strategies: initially, he denied there were any problems concerning Jewish refugees desiring entry to the United States. When this policy was exposed as a lie, he then testified that everything that could be done was already being done. Another lie. Long was dismissed from his post in 1944. General George S. Patton, a more publicly recognizable figure, was a war hero. A masterful military strategist, he was a fervent antisemite. He wrote in his diary that displaced Jews were "locusts," "lower than animals," and "a subhuman species without any of the cultural or social refinements of our times."[20] There seemed an inverse proportion between his intense military prowess and his unrelenting dislike of Jews; the greater his battlefield triumphs, the more credence was given to his contempt for Jews.

General Dwight D. Eisenhower, Supreme Commander of the Allied Expeditionary Force in Europe, had a different attitude. He ordered a visual documentary of the scene at Ohrdruf concentration camp, part of the Buchenwald camp complex, which American soldiers liberated. Charred corpses were strewn about the area, prisoners suffering from starvation and disease were lying on the ground, and the stench of death was omnipresent. Eisenhower wanted a visual record in case some people in the future were ever to deny the existence of death camps and the Holocaust. In Eisenhower's singularly prescient words:

> The same day I saw my first horror camp . . . I visited every nook and cranny . . . because I felt it my duty to be in a position from then on to testify about these things in case there ever grew up at home the belief or assumption that "the stories of Nazi brutality were just propaganda."[21]

Eisenhower became a de facto witness. The visual record he ordered appears on the top floor of the United States Holocaust Memorial Museum. He also cabled General George C. Marshall, Army Chief of Staff, for permission to bring members of Congress and journalists to the camps so that they could bear witness of the terrible truth to the American people. President Truman himself granted this request. The deprivation experienced in the death camps is perhaps summarized in Wiesel's image of man as a "starved stomach." There are of course countless other examples, such as a father beaten to death by his son for the former's crust of bread. The son was in turn murdered by other prisoners for the precious ration. Stories of torture, deprivation, and cruelty suffuse the pages of Wiesel's memoir.

Wiesel was unsparing in his criticism of American Jewry's failure to do more to rescue their European Jewish brethren, although he contended that his role was that of witness and not judge. He had suffered great cruelty during the Holocaust and had lost over half of his immediate family. The question of rescue is a vexing issue. Wiesel of course viewed historical events through a moral lens. He was not a trained historian but in his view the matter of responsibility involved first and foremost moral obligation. Other considerations were secondary. On the one hand, President Roosevelt continually mouthed the slogan "Rescue through victory." Near the end of the war Rabbi Stephen S. Wise, a strong supporter of the president and an articulate spokesperson for American Jewry, admonished Roosevelt that if he waited until military victory, there would be no Jews left to rescue. The issue of Roosevelt's concern for the Jews during the Holocaust is a complex and multilayered matter. On the one hand, in their 2013 book entitled *FDR and the Jews*,[22] Richard Breitman and Allan J. Lichtman argue for the existence of four Roosevelts. He was a bystander in his first term. During his second term he attended to Jewish concerns including loosening immigration restrictions via executive powers and a plan to resettle European Jews elsewhere. In his third incarnation FDR's activism diminished amid concerns over Hitler and military planning for war. He did not wish to be perceived as fighting a war for the Jews. In his final term, Roosevelt sought to address Jewish concerns with revived interest. He gave a speech in which he claimed, "There is no place in the lives and thoughts of true Americans for Antisemitism."[23]

There was the possibility of "rescue" if one means by "rescue" an attempt to bomb the railroad tracks leading to Auschwitz. The argument against this at the time was that these tracks could be repaired quickly and there was an abundance of slave labor to do this task. While this is true, the failure to bomb the tracks was also a signal to Hitler that the Western world did not care what he did to the Jews. Similarly, with the firebombing of Dresden, no leaflets were dropped with the message, "This is in partial retaliation to what you are doing to the Jews." It is also worth noting that during the 1938 Evian Conference held by the Allies to rescue Jews from Hitlerian Europe, no country agreed to take in any Jewish refugees.

Breitman and Lichtman correctly observe that it was "far easier for Nazis to kill than for any outside power to intervene."[24] Hitler's war against the Jews was a spectacular success. His military war against the allies was an abysmal failure. The authors summarize FDR's response to the Jewish plight in writing that the cautious wartime president was "politically and emotionally stingy"[25] when it came to the Jewish situation. In fairness it should be noted that of the great powers, America, England, France, Russia, and the Vatican, it is true that FDR did the best, but this is not saying very much.[26]

Great Britain did permit the Kindertransport effort, which rescued 10,000 Jewish children, among them the writer Lore Siegel, the psychologist Dr. Ruth Westheimer, and the philosopher Geoffrey Hartman. In the United States, the 1,000 Children Project (OTC) was far less organized. The OTC received no U.S. government visa immigrant assistance. In 1939, Senator Robert F. Wagner and Representative Edith Rogers co-sponsored the Wagner/Rogers bill in Congress. The goal of the bill was to admit 20,000 unaccompanied Jewish child refugees into the United States. The bill died in a Congressional committee. Finally, Varian Fry, an American Protestant, and journalist, was sent by the emergency rescuing committee directed by Eleanor Roosevelt to Marseilles. His mission was to rescue Jewish intellectuals and artists. After 13 months, Fry was recalled, owing to the State Department's deliberate effort to shut down his mission. However, he did manage to the artist Marc Chagall, the intellectual Hannah Arendt, and the writer Leon Feuchtwanger. Fry is the sole American designated by Yad Vashem (Israel's National Museum and Memorial to Holocaust victims) as one of the "Righteous Among the Nations" who saved Jewish lives solely out of altruistic reasons.

The situation grows more complex when one takes into account the fact that Peter Bergson, also known as Hillel Kook, began an extensive speaking campaign designed to gain support for Europe's doomed Jews. Kook was the nephew of the first chief rabbi of Palestine. Bergson formed the Bergson group, which was comprised of a group of talented speakers. His efforts were opposed by the American Jewish Committee, which perceived him as a right-wing extremist, as opposed to the Labor Party, which was viewed by most American Jews as more liberal and more mainstream.

Bergson was a revisionist Zionist, one of a number of speakers stationed in America during the war. A representative of the right-wing Jewish Palestinian Irgun, which was in conflict with the mainstream centrist Haganah, forerunner of the Israeli Defense Forces. He tirelessly promoted Zionism and gave countless speeches seeking to raise awareness about the murder of European Jewry, and to raise a Jewish army to fight against Nazism.

Moreover, on July 21, 1942, a rally was held at Madison Square Garden in support of European Jewry and against the Hitlerian regime. An official message from President Franklin D. Roosevelt vowing to preserve democracy and defeat the Nazis and Axis powers was read. In addition, Chaim Weizmann, who would become Israel's first president, spoke at a 1943 Madison Square Garden rally in support of the Jewish people.

But in the final analysis Roosevelt remained unmoved and did as little as possible to ease the persecution of European Jewry.[27]

Wiesel's criticism appears valid, to an extent. Professor Sarna helpfully distinguishes between America's Judeophobia and Jewish organizational life. The former, as we have seen, was strongly rooted in and regularly expressed by American culture. The latter was also on public display, only heading in a vastly different direction. In addition to the aforementioned Madison Square Garden rallies, there were, for example, several days of mourning and prayer organized by various rabbis.[28] In one such observance, New York City's Mayor Fiorello LaGuardia, who was fluent in Yiddish, actively participated. But the nub of the rescue issue can be understood as a race between Hitler's determination to exterminate the Jewish people and those who wanted to stop the murder machine. Short of assassinating Hitler, what could the American Jewish community have done?[29] In addition, the Jewish community was fractured into several competing groups. The community lacked the political power and authority to respond effectively. Moreover, Jews as a group did not have the self-confidence to undertake such a mission in a coherent manner. Looking back on the situation, one can appreciate the Yiddish observation that in those dark days, America's Jews believed in three *Velts* (worlds): *Yenemsvelt* (the world to come), this *velt* (the present world), and Roosevelt.[30] While it is true that FDR had more Jews in his administration than all previous administrations combined, these people were what the historian Henry Feingold called "Sha Sha" Jews, who neither cared about nor advocated for Judaism. A primary reason for the exaggerated Jewish presence in FDR's administration was the fact that Jewish lawyers were excluded from employment by Wall Street's antisemitism. On the other hand, Wiesel reported that on the day of his liberation he "remembers one black sergeant, a muscled giant who wept tears of impotent rage and shame for the human species, when he saw us. He spewed curses that on his lips became holy words."[31] Wiesel would have an abiding affection for America for the rest of his life.

Responding to antisemitism, "liberal Jews and Christians," writes Sarna, came together under the framework of what would become the National Conference of Christians and Jews.[32] Having weathered the virulent antisemitic storm during the war years, interfaith efforts including in the military increased. By 1952, writes Sarna, "good Americans were supposed to be good Judeo-Christians. It was the new national creed."[33] The 1955 appearance of Will Herberg's *Protestant, Catholic, Jew* enshrined Judaism as one of the three communities of faith. For Herberg, to be an American meant to be either a Protestant, Catholic, or a Jew. America had become a "triple melting pot." As Sarna notes, despite ignoring any other religious group or secularists, Herberg's definition "captured the national imagination and shaped subsequent religious discourse."[34]

Wiesel from an early age exhibited the traits of a religiously committed individual thoroughly immersed in the teachings of sacred texts who fervently believed in the coming of the Messiah. As noted, for the teenaged Wiesel and two of his close friends, this meant engaging in rigorous ascetic practices including recitation of incantations prescribed by practical kabbalah (devotional mysticism) under the guidance of their teacher. These practices, intended to hasten the Messiah's arrival, failed to achieve their goal. We have already mentioned that two of Wiesel's friends suffered physically from this regimen. Nevertheless, Wiesel persisted. Deportation to Auschwitz halted these practices for the three teenagers. Years later, in the early 1950s following Wiesel's journey to India where he observed the lot of the "Untouchable" caste, he attested that suffering was not ennobling; it was degrading.

Wiesel's paradigm of holiness came under radical assault during the Shoah. His classic memoir *Night* (*La Nuit*, 1958, English translation 1960) traces the three-fold stages of the fate of Sighet's Jews: ghettoization, transportation to Auschwitz, and extermination. Illusion, notes Wiesel, ruled the ghetto. Responding to the Nazi decree that all Jews had to wear a yellow star, Shlomo Wiesel contended, "So what? It's not lethal." Wiesel adds parenthetically, "(Poor Father! Of what then did you die?)."[35] Deported on the eve of Passover, 1944, their journey has been described as an "anti-Exodus" moving from freedom to slavery, from order to chaos, from life to annihilation. Wiesel's memoir treats three sets of relationships: his relationship with God, with the teachings of traditional Judaism, and with his father, which reveal the extent of the Shoah's deadly assault against the fundamental pillars of Judaism's sacred canopy. Wiesel writes in *Night* of Yom Kippur (the most solemn of Jewish holy days) in Auschwitz:

> I did not fast. First of all, to please my father who had forbidden me to do so. And then, there was no longer any reason for me to fast. I no longer accepted God's silence. As I swallowed my ration of soup, I turned that act into a symbol of rebellion, of protest against Him.

Wiesel frequently attested that his memoir begins where Anne Frank's diary ended. The collective effect of Nazism's war against the Jews ultimately led Wiesel to a life of defiant activism in America and elsewhere. See Chapter 5.

POST-LIBERATION, POST-SHOAH JEWISH IDENTITY

Following liberation, Wiesel had no desire to return to Sighet. He and 400 other child survivors (all orphans) from Buchenwald were initially set to go to Belgium, but at the intervention of French President Charles De Gaulle, they went instead to France. They were cared for upon arrival by the O.S.E., L'Oeuvre de Secours aux Enfants, a French Jewish organization devoted to rescuing Jewish refugee children uprooted by the war, located in Normandy. While housed in the O.S.E. chateau, Wiesel requested pen and paper and began a private journal, which became the skeletal framework for *Night*. He belonged to a group of youthful believers who asked for kosher food and "essential" books: the Bible, prayer books, and several Talmudic tractates. Wiesel recovered his religious zeal, "guided," he attested, "by one certainty." However, much the world had changed, "the Talmudic universe was the same."[36] The 400 youthful survivors were divided into two groups: observant Jews (about 100) and the non-observant. The first group was transferred to the Chateau d'Ambloy, located in northwestern France.

Moving to Paris, Wiesel became a student, studying French literature, philosophy, and psychology at the Sorbonne and the University of Paris. He wrote the majority of his books in French, many of which were translated by his wife, Marion, whom he met in New York City where Wiesel was stationed as a correspondent for *Yediot Ahronot* The Wiesels were married in 1969 in Jerusalem and have a son, Elisha (born 1972), daughter-in-law, Lynn Bartner-Wiesel, and two grandchildren, Elijah and Shira. Wiesel told his then teenage son Elisha that he loved him, no matter his purple hair. Echoing Doyde Feig's words to him prior to the Shoah, Wiesel told his son; the important thing is to remain Jewish.

Wiesel also began reading non-Jewish sources and was influenced by the existentialists, especially the works of Albert Camus. Desperately poor, he supported himself through a variety of jobs: camp counselor, tutor, and translator. He also was a choir director—he loved music and had a marvelous voice. In the fall of 1997 I was privileged to be among a small group in his Boston University office when Wiesel sang a series of niggunim (wordless Hasidic melodies). In 1992 he gave a concert at the 92nd Street Y in New York. Additionally, Wiesel was a frequent visitor to France and kept in close touch with leading French intellectuals. He and French President François Mitterrand were close friends until it was revealed that the president had been associated for a time with the collaborationist René Bousquet of the Vichy government during the Holocaust.

It was during his student days in Paris that Wiesel met Shushani, a strange and mysterious figure who was rumored to know 30 languages and to have memorized the Talmud and the *Zohar* (Book of Splendor, a classic text of Jewish mysticism). He doubtless had a photographic memory. Lithuanian born, physically distinctive with a small fedora perched on his large head, dust-filled eyeglass lenses, unkempt and poorly dressed, and cynical, his real name was probably Mordechai Rosenbaum, whose father took him around Europe where he would perform his prodigious memory feats.[37] Shushani also tutored the French philosopher Emmanuel Levinas, among others. Wiesel reported that he was preparing to lecture on the Book of Job when a mysterious stranger said, "Poor Job. Hasn't he suffered enough without your misinterpretation?" Shushani then proceeded to deliver a brilliant lecture on Job which left the audience, and Wiesel, dumbfounded. Wiesel observeed of Shushani: "I don't know if he was a holy man in disguise, a kabbalist wandering the earth to gather 'divine sparks' so as to reconstitute the original flame, or an eternal vagabond, the timeless outsider who embodies doubt and threat."[38]

Shushani would arrive at Wiesel's nearly barren room unannounced, and begin his instruction. He would then disappear, reappearing only according to his own timetable. Wiesel attested that "it is to him I owe my constant drive to question, my pursuit of the mystery that lies within knowledge and of the darkness hidden within light." Moreover, Shushani's teaching had a profound impact on Wiesel's Jewish identity. "What I do know," writes Wiesel, "is that I would not be the man I am, the Jew I am, had not an astonishing disconcerting vagabond accosted me one day to inform me that I understood nothing."[39] Wiesel's life-long insistence on the importance of questions owes much to the tutoring of Shushani.

Wiesel had other transformative encounters in Paris. He studied French under the tutelage of François Wahl, "an excellent teacher," and met many of the country's leading intellectuals and publishers. His initial meeting with Nobel Laureate in Literature François Mauriac in 1955 was clearly among these life-altering encounters. It inaugurated the first authentic post-Holocaust Jewish-Christian dialogue of Wiesel's life. Interviewing Mauriac in his Paris apartment, the young journalist listened as the older writer confided how deeply the image of cattle cars filled with Jewish children at the Austerlitz train station moved him. In fact, it was Mauriac's wife who had seen this abomination and reported it to her husband. Wiesel responded, "I was one of them." Growing impatient with Mauriac's constant reference to the suffering of Jesus, Wiesel responded: "Sir, I knew Jewish children, every one of whom suffered a thousand times more, six million times more, than Christ on the cross. And we don't speak about them. Can you understand that, sir? We don't speak about them."[40] Wiesel then angrily stormed out of Mauriac's apartment.

The old writer followed Wiesel, asking him to come back. Mauriac wept and asked Wiesel to continue. "Yes, I have lived through *those events*. Yes, I have known the sealed trains. Yes, I have seen darkness cover man's faith. Yes, I was present at the end of the world."[41] Mauriac told Wiesel that he was wrong not to speak. "Listen to the old man that I am: one must speak out—one must *also* speak out."[42] One year later Wiesel sent him the manuscript of *Night*. Mauriac himself took the manuscript to various publishers. His Foreword appears in every edition of the 30 languages in which the memoir has been published.

In the years between the late '50s and the mid-'60s Wiesel traveled extensively—to South America, multiple times to Israel, to Russia twice, and to Europe, from 1958–1968. He became a reporter for the Israeli paper *Yediot Ahronot* and a contributor to the American (*Forverts*). Yiddish for Foreward. During his early student days in Paris, and feeling the need to struggle for Palestine, Wiesel sought employment among the various Jewish agencies in the city. But as he later confessed in *All Rivers Run to the Sea*, he "didn't know one underground group from another." Furthermore, he noted that "if the gatekeeper at the Jewish agency hadn't turned me away, I might have been sitting at a desk working for the Haganah, translating an insulting article about the Irgun."[43] Wiesel was apolitical and focused his attention on writing. He was, like many others, disappointed and confused when David Ben Gurion ordered the sinking of the ship *Altalena* on the beaches of Tel Aviv. The ship had been carrying arms which the Irgun intended to use against the Haganah headed by Ben Gurion, Israel's first prime minister. Wiesel ultimately came to terms with this situation.

Following his 1955 move to New York where he was stationed as a correspondent for *Yedioth Ahronoth*, Wiesel was hit by a cab in 1958 and, severely injured, spent the better part of a year in a wheelchair. He wrote about this experience in his novel *The Accident* (French title *Le Jour, The Day*). The novel's intrigue centers on the fact that Wiesel might have contemplated suicide; the text hints that he glimpsed the oncoming cab. Wiesel himself said that the accident was a literary experiment exploring the possibility of suicide. Distinguishing Holocaust survivors from the American-born, Wiesel writes: "Our stay there [in the camps] planted time bombs within us. From time to time one of them explodes. . . . Anyone who has been there has brought back some of humanity's madness."[44] Writing for the *Forverts*, he contributed over 1,000 essays and reviews in Yiddish, some of which appeared under his pseudonym, Elisha Carmeli.

Yet Wiesel came in for scathing criticism from the ultraorthodox (Yiddish speakers) who opposed both his questioning of God after the Shoah as well as all interfaith efforts. Shortly before his death, Wiesel criticized then presidential candidate Trump's election campaign call for a Muslim ban. In response *Yiddish Moment*, an ultraorthodox newspaper, wrote the following several months before the election: "Such actions make the old duck into a legitimate target. The mumkhe-hagodl (great expert), who has gebarabanyevet (drummed on) about the Shoah. . . , is defending jackals as diabolical as the Nazis."[45] Furthermore, the same paper wrote, "He's a *vizele* [a little weasel], who's made an entire career thanks to the *Khurban*," Holocaust, and "the epitome of the actor who won't get off the stage after the audience has long left the theatre."[46] This type of critique is clearly *ad hominem* but still reveals the rift between Wiesel's point of view that he is not God's policeman and the theological triumphalism of the ultraorthodox Hasidim, who clearly believe that they are.

NIGHT AND THE ARGUING WITH GOD TRADITION

In Judaism God is both Judge and judged. The Master of the Universe is a deity with whom one can—and must—dispute. Arguing with God is a feature of biblical, rabbinic, and Hasidic Jewish theology. Abraham, Moses and the prophets, Job, and Jeremiah all engage in this interrogation, as does Hasidic Judaism. Rabbi Anson Laytner dubs this the "Law Court pattern of prayer." Arguing with God, attests Laytner, "is a particularly (and perhaps uniquely) Jewish response to the problem of theodicy."[47] Since injustice does exist, God can, as it were, be "sued and justice demanded."[48] Translating this to Wiesel's position, it is not surprising to hear the Nobel laureate contend that "as a Jew you will sooner or later be confronted with the enigma of God's action in history. Without God, Jewish existence would intrigue only the sociologists. With him, it both fascinates and baffles philosophers and theologians."[49] In this sense, Wiesel is heir to a long-established tradition, although his disputation with the deity is, at the same time, distinctive. Abraham negotiates with God over the fate of Sodom's inhabitants (Genesis 18:16–33). The deity is set to destroy the city, owing to its inhabitants' immoral ways. Abraham intercedes, querying

God on moral grounds, "Shall not the Judge of all the earth do right?" (Genesis 18:25, King James Version). Stated in its simplest and most morally profound sense, the question is: why should the righteous be destroyed along with the wicked?

Abraham inquires of the deity, what if you can find 50 righteous; will you annul your decree? Following a series of negotiations, God finally agrees to spare the city if even ten righteous are found. But they cannot be found. The point of this story is not that God destroyed Sodom. The point is that Abraham, despite his fear—"Behold I have taken upon myself to speak to the Lord, I who am but dust and ashes" (Genesis 18:27)—is able to be God's interlocutor.

JEREMIAH, JOB, MOSES

The prophet Jeremiah, one of Wiesel's favorite biblical figures, asks the fundamental question concerning theodicy: "Why does the way of the wicked prosper? Why do all who are treacherous thrive?" (Jeremiah 12:1). Like Jeremiah, Wiesel also accompanied the Jewish people into exile, where he persisted in posing his questions about the apparent lack of divine justice while the wicked prosper. Job treats the issue of the suffering of innocents based on his personal experience. He doubts not God's existence but rather divine justice. In terms of the Law Court pattern, Job is portrayed as the plaintiff and God as the defendant. In *Night* Wiesel writes, "I concurred with Job! I was not denying His [God's] existence, but I doubted His absolute justice."[50] Moses intercedes with God on behalf of the Israelites. He persuades God to annul His own decree against His own people. Far from being angry with Moses, the Lord of the universe rewards him, giving him the second set of tablets which contain both the written and oral law.

The Hasidic movement has a long tradition of arguing with God. Levi Yitzhak of Berditchev (1740–1809) is perhaps the best-known proponent of this approach, although it is recorded that he never won any of his arguments with the deity. Nevertheless, Wiesel writes of him: "His most beautiful adventures, the most beautiful accounts and stories of his adventures, are those that show him in his role of attorney for the defense, challenging and remonstrating the Judge." Elsewhere, the Berditchever, addressing God, said: "When a Jew sees *tephillin* [phylacteries] on the ground, he runs to pick them up and kisses them. Isn't it written that we are Your *tephillin*? Are you never going to lift us toward you?"[51] Wiesel writes that as a child, "I loved his [adventures and stories] and saw in them nothing but love and friendship. Today I feel their weight of despair and revolt—and love them even more."[52] Consequently, Wiesel's extended *din Torah* (trial of God), which always occurs from *within* the tradition, rests on a long-established precedent.

NIGHT

Wiesel's foundational memoir is, attested its author, "both the end of everything and the beginning of everything." The memoir, which was featured in Oprah Winfrey's Book Club in 2006, problematizes the notion that God intervenes in history in order to protect His chosen people. History itself provides far too many instances of counter examples to this contention; the two destructions of the Jerusalem Temple, persecution in foreign lands, pogroms, the seventeenth-century Chmielnicki uprising, and, *within* the Jewish tradition, the theological chaos caused by two false messiahs, Shabbatai Tzvi (seventeenth century) and Jacob Joseph Frank (eighteenth century). And yet, Judaism continued despite these obstacles. The Holocaust in the twentieth century is the ultimate touchstone for evil that implicates God. How to speak of God's justice amid a history which apparently reveals that God is either powerless or indifferent? Can a religious community endure in the face of such "hideous wounding"? Wiesel inquired, what has happened to the God of our ancestors? How is it possible to speak of God after the Holocaust?

Wiesel was keenly aware that one cannot thank God for Jerusalem while ignoring Treblinka. To do so is hypocritical. "And yet," to employ Wiesel's signature phrase, the matter does not end here. As a mystic, Wiesel embraced paradox. Faith, for him, meant that although one has every right to cease believing, one continues to believe. Reflecting the influence of Camus, Wiesel contended in a world without apparent meaning, one must endlessly strive to create meaning. Wiesel was a writer who was a witness to and lived in exile.[53] See Arthur Green "Wiesel in the Context of Neo-Hasidism in *Elie Wiesel: Jewish, Literary, and Moral Perspectives.* Edited by Steven T. Katz and Alan L. Rosen. Blooomington: Indiana University Press, 2013 page 55.

As such he voiced the aspiration of both communal and personal existence. But he did so only after undergoing his own "dark night of the soul."

Night questions classical Jewish teachings. Reversing the *Akedah* (Binding of Isaac), Wiesel's memoir portrays sons abandoning fathers. Another scene has a group of Jewish prisoners saying the *kaddish* (prayer for the dead) *for themselves.* Again, Wiesel in *Night* becomes God's accuser—"I felt very strong. I was the accuser, God the accused. . . . I felt myself stronger than this Almighty to whom my life had been bound for so long."[54] The author's central position is a protest against God who, while intervening to save a Jewish child from being bricked into an Egyptian pyramid by order of the Pharaoh, failed to intervene on behalf of the one and a half million Jewish children murdered in the Shoah.[55] Nevertheless, Wiesel was a protestor who remains *within* the Jewish tradition. Responding to an interviewer, Wiesel attested,

> I would use the adjective *wounded*, which I believe may be valid for every-
> one in my generation. Hasidism teaches that no heart is as whole as a broken
> heart, and I would say that no faith is as solid as a wounded faith.[56]

Three events, each successively severe, from his memoir deserve attention.
First is the author's shattering acknowledgment, during his first night in
Auschwitz, of Nazism's radical assault against his traditional image of the
God of history:

> Never shall I forget that night, the first night in camp, that
> Turned my life into one long night seven times sealed.
> . . . Never shall I forget the small faces of the children whose bodies
> I saw transformed into smoke under a silent sky.
> Never shall I forget those flames that consumed my faith for-
> Ever. . .
>   Never shall I forget those moments that murdered my God
> And my soul and turned my dreams to ashes.
> Never shall I forget those things, even were I condemned to
> Live as long as God Himself.
> Never.[57]

Wiesel's embrace of paradox is clear when he speaks both of his "murdered
God," and being "condemned to live as long as God Himself." Anson Laytner contends that for Wiesel, paradox is the most apt way of expressing the
post-Holocaust Jewish experience, "one in which the relationship between
God and Israel remains unchanged and yet radically different."[58] Further,
this paradox is particularly applicable to what post-Holocaust Jews ur-
gently desire: "The experience of the Holocaust demanded a confrontation
with God."[59]

Second, further on in his memoir Wiesel notes that he had become a
different person. "The student of Talmud, the child I was, had been consumed by the flames. All that was left was a shape that resembled me. My
soul had been invaded—and devoured—by a black flame."[60]

Third is the hanging of three Jewish prisoners in Auschwitz

Three prisoners, two adults and a young boy, were sentenced to be
hanged in Auschwitz for plotting a revolt. The other prisoners were
ordered to march past the gallows. The two adults were dead, but the
child, too light, was still breathing. He remained that way for half an hour.
A prisoner behind Wiesel asked, "For God's sake, where is God?" Wiesel
responded, "Where He is? This is where—hanging from this gallows."[61]
This scene has been widely mischaracterized. God did not literally die, but
the innocence of the child, which stands for the existence of divine justice, compels a radical re-imaging of God and the deity's role in history.
This is the dilemma confronting the late twentieth-century believer, noted

Wiesel. By "allowing [the Holocaust] to happen, God was telling humanity something, and we don't know what it was. That He suffered? He could have—should have—interrupted His own suffering by calling a halt to the martyrdom of innocents."[62]

CRITIQUES OF *NIGHT*

Two American literary critics have leveled sensationalistic accusations against Wiesel's memoir. Alfred Kazin and Naomi Seidman have each attacked Wiesel and his book. I do not subscribe to either of their attacks. Alfred Kazin, who initially favorably reviewed *Night*, and who accompanied Yankel Rosensaft and his wife on a pilgrimage to Bergen-Belsen in 1970, has since taken to attack not only Wiesel, but his former friend Saul Bellow and Jerzy Kosinski as well.[63] The same situation occurred when Kazin began attacking the Jewish-American writer Hugh Nissenson.[64] Wiesel attested that "When . . . several of my books had found readers, he did what he could to turn them away."[65] Kazin evidently distrusted survivors, although this did not stop him from accepting their generosity (see note 63).

Kazin's most damning charge against Wiesel was the accusation that he invented the episode in *Night* describing the three inmates who were hanged together. Wiesel responded with the question: "How dare he?"[66] Wiesel was outraged by the nerve of Kazin in questioning this seminal act which, he contended, gave comfort to Holocaust deniers. Thousands witnessed the event, some of whom are still alive. Wiesel listed the names of the three victims: Leo Yehuda Diamond, the youngest, and the two adults, Nathan Weisman and Yanek Grossfeld. Finally, Wiesel pointed to the difference between Kazin and himself in terms of the concept of writing. For Kazin, literature is "an end in itself." For Wiesel, however, post-Shoah there can be no art for art's sake. Testimonial literature's goal is to disturb. Wiesel disturbed

> the believer because I dare to put questions to God . . . I disturb the miscreant because, despite my doubts and questions, I refuse to break with the religious and mystical universe that has shaped my own. . . . If I have learned anything in my life, it is to distrust intellectual comfort.[67]

A controversy has also arisen concerning the difference in the Yiddish, French, and English translations of *Night*. Naomi Seidman alleges that Wiesel intentionally toned down the anger in the initial Yiddish version (*Un di Velt Hot Geshvign*, 1956). Furthermore, she contends that the shortened French version (*La Nuit*, 1958) differs substantially from the Yiddish. Wiesel, she attests, downplayed the anger in the Yiddish to make the

French more amenable to non-Jewish readers.[68] Wiesel addressed some of these differences among the versions of *Night* in the introduction to the 2006 translation by Marion Wiesel. I do not believe that Seidman's critique is an adequate or fair criticism for two reasons: it omits the impact of the passage of time on Wiesel's consciousness, and it overlooks the normative Jewish theological position of arguing with God, which I discuss later.

Seidman's criticism centers on her belief that Wiesel must have thought that Jewish rage would be unacceptable to a Christian audience. Professor Margarete Myers Feinstein instead attests that Wiesel's attitude had changed. Wiesel himself acknowledged this in observing that he would have used more temperate language if writing later, although he was still unwilling to let God off the theological hook.

Feinstein attests that over time some of those who had engaged in revenge (believing that) "all Germans should suffer came to revise their opinions and distinguished between war criminals and ordinary German citizens"[69] Furthermore, she makes a helpful distinction between *revenge* characterized by resentment, and *vengeance*, which is associated with moral outrage and anger.[70] Combing through survivor oral history interviews, Feinstein makes another crucial observation in distinguishing gender responses. Some males did shoot Nazis. But they refrained from violence against German women. Concerning Wiesel's position, Feinstein notes that "it seems plausible . . . that sometime before 1962, Wiesel began letting go of his hatred for Germans."[71] In *The Fifth Son*, Wiesel attested that vengeance is God's prerogative. This leads to a moral struggle to "the realization that survivors can use words to serve justice in this world."[72] Wiesel's works illuminate a realization that "Jewish rage no longer demanded revenge. It demanded justice." Wiesel did not soften his position to avoid offending Christians. Far more likely is his theological maturation over time, especially in his attestation that all hatred ultimately leads to self-hatred.

Turning to Wiesel's novel *The Fifth Son*, Feinstein notes that Ariel, the second "only son" of Holocaust survivors, learns that his father's obsession with vengeance stems from the fact that the father had participated in the execution of a Nazi commandant who had ordered the murder of the European-born Ariel. The son thinks that in those days that was the thing to do. This conforms to the position Wiesel took in the Yiddish version, "that the mitzvah of vengeance be fulfilled."[73] However, the post-war Ariel learns the commandant is still alive. He determines to complete the mission, seeking a blessing from a Hasidic rebbe who teaches him that traditional Judaism requires that vengeance be left to God.

The son confronts the former Nazi in his luxurious West German office. Abandoning his intended mission, the son instead will unmask the man:

"Wherever you are you shall feel like an intruder, pursued by the dead. . . . Men will think of you with revulsion; they will curse you like the plague and war; they will curse you when they curse death."[74] What had seemed desirable in the immediate aftermath of the war was no longer acceptable. "Telling the story, robbing the murderers of their comfortable lives is the path to this worldly justice."[75]

Wiesel offered other images of God throughout his voluminous writings: God makes fun of human beings, his favorite toys (*The Accident*); God is imprisoned! Man must free Him (*The Town Beyond the Wall*); God is guilty. He has become the ally of evil, of death, of murder. . . . "I ask you a question and dare you answer:" "What is there left for us to do?" (*The Gates of the Forest*); the human image supplants that of God—man is increasingly responsible for redemption (*A Beggar in Jerusalem*); the road to God leads through man (*Souls on Fire*); God awaits redemption through His creatures (*The Accident, The Town Beyond the Wall, The Gates of the Forest, The Oath*). Elsewhere, Wiesel wrote both that God can take care of Himself and that only God is alone; humans need other humans, and that God is a wounded deity (*Memoirs: All Rivers Run to the Sea*). Wiesel told an interviewer that following the Hasidic teaching that no heart is as whole as a broken heart: "I would say that no faith is as solid as a wounded faith."[76]

Wiesel's argument with God undercuts the two traditional Jewish responses to theodicy—"We are punished for our sins," and "Suffering as a proof of Love"—while maintaining the imperative of interrogating the deity. *Ani Ma'amanim* (1973) is a cantata based on Maimonides' twelfth assertion, "I believe with perfect faith in the coming of the Messiah even though he may tarry." This cantata is a revision of the midrashic legend found in *Lamentations Rabbah*. Wiesel portrays each of the three patriarchs Abraham, Isaac, and Jacob appealing to God as the Jewish people undergo the agony of the Holocaust. Receiving no response, they return to earth to be with the Jewish people. What the patriarchs do not know is that God sheds a tear and follows them, "weeping, smiling, whispering: *Nitzhuni banai*, my children have defeated me, they deserve my gratitude." Laytner makes the point that the deity Wiesel portrays here is not "a remote omnipotent God but an anthropopathic God in need of human redemption."[77]

Wiesel's play *The Trial of God* appeared six years after his cantata. The volume is a *purim schpiel* (Purim play) which occurs shortly after a violent pogrom in an obscure mid-seventeenth-century village named Shamgorod. Three traveling minstrels arrive in the village. It was decided to put God on trial for permitting His children to be massacred. Berish, the innkeeper, whose daughter had been raped and can no longer speak, is God's accuser. After an apparently futile search to find someone to speak in God's defense, a mysterious stranger named Sam steps forward. Maria, a servant girl at the inn, warns the others that Sam is actually Satan and had seduced her. Mendel, one of the three minstrels, serves as judge. He frequently asks, "And God in all of this?" An antisemitic priest offers the Jews an escape plan, which involves conversion, but they decline. Berish voices the Jewish argument with God:

> He annihilated Shamgorod and you want me to be for Him?
> I can't! If He insists upon going on with His methods, let Him
> —but I won't say Amen. Let Him crush me, I won't say
> Kaddish. Let Him kill me, let Him kill us all, I shall shout and
> Shout that it's His fault. I'll use my last energy to make my
> Protest known. Whether I live or die, I submit to Him no
> Longer.[78]

THE DEATH OF GOD DEBATE IN AMERICA

The '60s in America was a time of cultural, political, and theological upheaval. Five political assassinations shook the country: Medgar Evers, Malcom X, President John F. Kennedy, Martin Luther King, and Attorney General Robert F. Kennedy all were slain between 1963 and 1968. In addition, and not to be forgotten, were the murders of many less famous people in the Deep South owing to segregation and racism. Perhaps the most famous were four black children: Addie Mae Collins, Cynthia Wesley, Carole Robertson, and Denise McNair were murdered when their Birmingham, Alabama, church was bombed in 1963. Three civil rights workers were murdered: one African American, James Chaney, and two Jews, Andrew Goodman and Michael Schwerner, in Philadelphia, Mississippi, in 1964. An Italian American woman from Detroit, Viola Liuzzo, was murdered in Alabama in 1965.

Protests against the war in Vietnam, civil rights demonstrations, race riots, and the Cuban missile crisis added to feelings of rage and uncertainty. America also landed a man on the moon at the decade's end. Gas cost 35 cents a gallon in 1969, and one could purchase a new home for about $28,000. As we have noted, traditional religious explanations for theodicy were found wanting, Eastern religions exercised great fascination, and the impulse to be free of constraints was seen in movements as disparate as the woman's liberation movement and the embrace of Eastern religiosity. It is against this background that the death of God movement emerged. Initially this movement appeared in Protestant religious circles and was articulated most prominently by Thomas J.J. Altizer, William Hamilton, and Paul Van Buren. Collectively they argued that etymologically "religion" comes from Latin, meaning "to bind." Hence, the death of

God meant, for the Protestant theologians, the liberation of man. It was an event to be celebrated.

Wiesel's prize-winning novel *A Beggar in Jerusalem* reflects on the cultural and theological significance of the 1967 Six Day War. Wiesel went to Israel during this war, which Israel decisively won. The novel takes place shortly after the war and weaves back and forth in terms of time. *A Beggar in Jerusalem* is a literary statement of the role of God and man in Jewish history. Wiesel linked the Holocaust with Israel's lightning-like victory in observing that Israel won because it could deploy six million more souls in its battle. Beggars are an omnipresent feature of Wiesel's novels and can represent the tradition's relationship to its past. They also may, in fact, be viewed as Elijah-like figures.

The Jewish death of God movement was far more nuanced, offering not liberation but eternal questions about God, about the sacred canopy, and about the nature of Judaism. The feeling here was not one of celebration but rather sorrow. Discussing Wiesel's understanding of the death of God movement in comparison with the position of Richard L. Rubenstein and Michael Berenbaum provides insight into each of these thinkers as well as the state of American culture at the time. The literary dimension of each position is viewed through a theological lens. During the '60s alone, Wiesel published eight volumes: *Night* (1960), *Dawn* (1961), *The Accident* (1962), *The Town Beyond the Wall* (1964), *The Gates of the Forest* (1964), *The Jews of Silence* (1966), *Legends of Our Time* (1968), and *A Beggar in Jerusalem* (1968). In addition, he gave an endless series of public lectures both in America and abroad and spoke to overflow crowds at the 92nd Street Y and in his annual public lecture series at Boston University. Addressing a variety of topics—Hasidism, Jesus, American Judaism, Israel—the Holocaust informed the central topic with its stress on the importance of Holocaust memory.

Wiesel's first three volumes led him further away from the covenantal portrayal of a deity who is also the Lord of history. Wiesel, Rubenstein, and Berenbaum all concur that the Holocaust was an unprecedented event in Jewish history, one that compels analysis of the impact of the death camps and their relationship to the traditional image of God as the Lord of history. For each thinker the Law Court pattern became, along with the Jewish people, victims of the Shoah. God either died, became replaced by the idea of the void, or was wounded by Auschwitz. Moreover, each thinker developed a specific image of God that was tested by what American culture was willing to embrace.

Richard L. Rubenstein, one of America's pre-eminent theologians of culture, an ordained rabbi, and a Harvard PhD, was a chaired professor of religion at Florida State University (1970–1995). Leaving FSU, he became president of the University of Bridgeport and professor of religion prior to his retiring. His 1966 book *After Auschwitz* inaugurated discussion on the meaning of the Holocaust for religious thought in both Judaism and Christianity. But it is important to remember that for Rubenstein, the death of God was a cultural fact. No man can convincingly claim that God is dead. Rather, all constraints, moral, ethical, political, and religious, had been removed by the extermination of six million Jewish people. "No modern King David," wrote Rubenstein, "need fear being rebuked by a Nathan the prophet." Moreover, Rubenstein self-identified as a Pagan. This means "to find once again one's roots as a child of Earth and to see one's own existence as wholly and totally an earthly existence."[79] Rubenstein continues, "For mankind the true divinities are the gods of earth, not the high gods of the sky; the gods of space and place, not the gods of time; the gods of home and hearth, not the gods of wandering."[80] Nature, rather than history, is the arena in which human destiny is played out.

Rubenstein expressly stated what he meant by saying we live in the time of the death of God. His statement deserves full citation.

> When I say we live in the time of the death of God,
> I mean that the thread uniting God and man, heaven
> And earth, has been broken. We stand in a cold, silent,
> Unfeeling cosmos, unaided by any purposeful power
> Beyond our own resources. After Auschwitz, what else
> Can a Jew say about God?[81]

It is, attests Rubenstein, very difficult to live in the universe without God. Rubenstein is, however, not an atheist. Rather he claims that religion remains a significant domain of human life when it comes to the rites of passage: birth, bar and bat mitzvoth, marriage, illness, and death. Essentially, Rubenstein emphasizes the priestly rather than the prophetic dimension of religion. Moreover, he advocated that history overwhelms and destroys claims about God's intervention on behalf of the chosen people. This led Rubenstein to the daring conclusion that the Jewish people should abandon the claim of chosenness. Rubenstein, a powerful thinker and lucid writer, despite the attention he garnered in scholarly circles, attracted very few followers.

In 1961 Rubenstein had a decisive interview with Dean Heinrich Grüber, who was the only German who had testified against Adolph Eichmann at his Jerusalem trial. Grüber had courageously aided Jews and other opponents of Nazism during the war and had been tortured and imprisoned in Dachau, where his teeth were knocked out. The interview took place against an apocalyptic background; the Soviets were putting up the infamous Berlin Wall, which divided the city into East and West sectors.

Grüber insisted on the collective guilt of Germans for the Holocaust. Following the Shoah, Grüber received many honorary degrees both in Europe and America. In addition, he was named one of the Righteous Among the Nations by Israel's Yad VaShem. Yet, he employed the framework of *heilsgeschichte* (holy or covenant history), which views historical events under the purview of God's sovereignty. This led him to claim that the Holocaust was implicitly divine punishment of the Jewish people. Rubenstein could not accept this position, which implied that God was either a cosmic sadist or powerless to stop the Shoah.

Wiesel responded to Rubenstein's position by stating two points which in fact were responses to Rubenstein's own query: "After Auschwitz, what else can a Jewish person say about God?" "How strange," asserted Wiesel, "that the philosophy denying God came not from the survivors. Those who came out with the so-called God is dead theology, not one of them had been in Auschwitz. Those who had never said it."[82] Wiesel had his problems with God: anger, quarrels, and nightmares. But, he continued, "my dispute, my bewilderment, my astonishment is with men."[83]

Wiesel's second point concerned Rubenstein's failure to understand survivors (like himself). It is, asserted Rubenstein, "more difficult to live today in a world without God." "NO!" attested Wiesel. "If you want difficulties, choose to live *with* God."[84] The tragedy of the believer cannot be compared to that of the nonbeliever. The believer is the one who confronts the real drama. Following this exchange, Rubenstein, as a rabbi, conferred his blessing on Wiesel. Wiesel's emphasis on tales which essentially are open ended and allow for the possibility of the tension between belief and doubt were received warmly by an American culture whose attitude toward God and religion was creatively ambiguous, permitting the widespread cultural embrace of the tension between faith and despair, as opposed to the finality of Rubenstein's death of God position.

Michael Berenbaum's 1979 volume *Elie Wiesel: God, the Holocaust, and the Children of Israel* is an insightful and well-researched analysis of Wiesel's thought and theological position within the context of selected Jewish thinkers. The author has served as director of the research institute of the United States Holocaust Memorial Museum, president and CEO of the Survivors of the Shoah Visual History Foundation, and director of the Sigi Ziering Institute of the American Jewish University. Originating as a PhD dissertation under the direction of Richard Rubenstein, Berenbaum's volume argues that Wiesel embraces traditional Judaism, even while challenging its central teachings. Consequently, he contends that Wiesel's theological vision is that of the void.

Discussing Wiesel's relationship to the God of traditional Judaism, Berenbaum, like Fine, notes that his first three volumes led him further away from the covenantal portrayal of a deity who is the Lord of history. Consequently, "Wiesel's titles become brighter as the presence of God becomes dimmer." Berenbaum continues, "This irony reflects Wiesel's reliance upon man in a world devoid of God."[85] Wiesel's activism and passion for social justice emerged from what Anson Laytner, a liberal rabbi who for many years directed the Jewish Federation Community Relations Council of Greater Seattle, describes as "defiant activism." However, Wiesel was also horrified by the depths of depravity to which humans can sink. Berenbaum observes that Wiesel's "desire to confront God [is] in order to vindicate humanity." Although Berenbaum argues that Wiesel's vision is one of a void, it is the case that Wiesel was thoroughly steeped in the cultural and religious tradition of Judaism. I contend that Wiesel's vision is less of a void than it is of a deity whose apparent absence in the death camps compels an ongoing search for a useable post-Holocaust image of the divine.

Discussing Wiesel's novel *The Gates of the Forest*, Berenbaum writes of Gregor that he shared with Wiesel "the desire to confront God in order to vindicate humanity."[86] This instantiates Wiesel's long-held contention that God must never be justified at the expense of man. In the same discussion, Berenbaum correctly notes that "traditions no longer mean what they once did." Nevertheless, "they allow one to reappropriate the past."[87] But in my view, Berenbaum stops too soon in writing "Wiesel is a heretic, albeit a heretic with profoundly Jewish memories and with a deep love and respect for tradition."[88] It is precisely this "deep love and respect for tradition" that prevents him from accepting a vision of God as the void.[89] It is not a void but rather more like an eclipse of God.[90] Wiesel himself contended on many occasions that if he were not still a believer, even if not in the same way he was prior to the Shoah, he would not continuously interrogate God. Chapter 2 addresses Wiesel's impact on post-Shoah Christian theologians and philosophers.

NOTES

1. Peter Berger, *The Sacred Canopy: Elements of a Sociological Theory of Religion*. New York: Anchor Books, 1969. See Chapter 1, "Religion and World Construction."
2. Ibid., page 45.
3. Maurice Friedman, *Abraham Joshua Heschel and Elie Wiesel: You are my Witnesses*. New York: Farrar-Straus-Giroux, 1987, page 163.
4. Elie Wiesel, *Night*. Translated by Marion Wiesel. New York: Hill and Wang, 2006, page 3.
5. Ibid., page 112.
6. Elie Wiesel, *All Rivers Run to the Sea*. New York: Alfred A. Knopf, 1995, page 363. Hereafter this work will be cited as *AR*.
7. Elie Wiesel, *A Jew Today*. Translated by Marion Wiesel. New York: Vintage Books, 1979, page 80.
8. Elie Wiesel, *Harry James Cargas in Conversation With Elie Wiesel*. New York: Indianapolis Books, 1992, page 85.

9. For an intelligent and far reaching discussion of traditional Hasidism, see Moshe Habertal, "The Dance Goes On," *New York Review of Books*, May 2018.

10. Elie Wiesel in discussion with my seminar students, March 2002.

11. Elie Wiesel, "Brooklyn: A New Hasidic Kingdom." Translated by Marion Wiesel. Elie Wiesel Collection, Gottleib Archive. Boston: Boston University Press, 1975, pages 12–13.

12. Ariel Burger, *Witness: Lessons From Elie Wiesel's Classroom*. Boston: Houghton Mifflin Harcourt, 2018, page 78.

13. Elie Wiesel, *Souls on Fire: Portraits and Legends of Hasidic Masters*. Translated by Marion Wiesel. New York: Random House, 1972, page 30. Hereafter this work will be cited as *Souls*.

14. Ibid., page 233.

15. Ibid., page 257.

16. Ibid., page 256.

17. Elie Wiesel, *And the Sea Is Never Full: Memoirs, 1969*. Translated by Marion Wiesel. New York: Alfred A. Knopf, 1999, page 168.

18. Miriam Sanua Dalin, *Let Us Prove Strong*. Hanover: University Press of New England, 2007, page 10.

19. Jonathan D. Sarna, *American Judaism: A History*. New Haven: Yale University Press, 2004, page 266. Hereafter this book will be cited as *AJ*.

20. M. Blumenson, *The Patton Papers 1940–1945*. Boston: Da Capo Press, 2009, pages 751, 787.

21. Dwight D. Eisenhower, *For the Dead and the Living, We Must Bear Witness*. United States Holocaust Memorial Council, postcard.

22. Richard Breitman and Allan J. Lichtman, *FDR and the Jews*. Cambridge: Harvard University Press, 2013.

23. Ibid., page 4.

24. Ibid., page 207.

25. Ibid., page 210.

26. Deputy Treasurer Secretary Hans Morgenthau's threat to expose FDR for foot dragging on the rescue issue is well known. However, historian Christopher Browning points out that in 1942 80% of Europe's Jews were alive. One year later, 20% remained after the most fatal year of the war. President Roosevelt did not assist European Jewry.

27. See the devastating critique of Roosevelt's Jewish policy in Rafael Medoff, *Franklin D. Roosevelt, Rabbi Stephen S. Wise and the Holocaust*. Philadelphia: Jewish Publications Society, 2019.

28. Henry Feingold writes that in the absence of assassinating Hitler, the American Jewish community could do very little. Arguments based on moral persuasion were not going to move the murderer. Feingold, "Did American Jewry Do Enough During the Holocaust?" in *Judaism in the Modern World*. Edited by Alan L. Berger. New York: New York University Press, 1944, pages 153–155.

29. Told to me by Yaffa Eliach in September 1996.

30. *AR*, page 97.

31. *AJ*, page 266.

32. Ibid., page 267.

33. Ibid., page 275.

34. Ibid.

35. Elie Wiesel, *Night*, page 11.

36. *AR*, page 113.

37. Ibid., page 129. Wiesel terms Shushani "a formidable acrobat of knowledge," page 129.

38. Ibid., page 125.

39. Ibid., page 130.

40. Wiesel, *A Jew Today*, page 13.

41. Ibid., page 23.

42. Ibid.

43. *AR*, page 163.

44. Elie Wiesel, "The Accident," in *The Night Trilogy*. Translated by Anne Borchardt. New York: Hill and Wang, 1990, page 303.

45. Alan Astro, *PowerPoint*. Dallas, TX: Ackerman Center for Holocaust Studies, March 2018.

46. Ibid.

47. Anson Laytner, *Arguing With God: A Jewish Tradition*. Northvale, NJ: Jason Aronson Inc., 1990, page xv. Hereafter this volume will be cited as *AG*.

48. Ibid., page xx.

49. Elie Wiesel: "To a Young Jew of Today," in *One Generation After*. Translated by Lily Edelman and Elie Wiesel. New York: Schocken Books, 1985, page 166.

50. Elie Wiesel, *Night*, page 45.

51. *Souls*, page 110.

52. Ibid., page 2002 page 104.

53. See Alan L. Berger, "Elie Wiesel: Writer as Witness to and in Exile," in *Exile in Global Literature and Culture: Homes Found and Lost*. Edited by Asher Z. Milbauer and James M. Sutton. New York: Routledge, 2020, pages 102–116. Camus' influence on Wiesel is ubiquitous, perhaps nowhere as striking as in Wiesel's statement: "When I look around the world I see nothing but hopelessness. And yet I must, try to find a source for hope. We must believe in human beings in spite of human beings." Robert Franciosi (editor), *Elie Wiesel: Conversations*. Jackson: University Press of Mississippi.

54. Elie Wiesel, *Night*, page 68.

55. Louis Ginzberg, *The Legends of the Jews*. Translated by Henrietta Szold. Baltimore: The John Hopkins University Press, 1998, Volume 2, page 299.

56. Elie Wiesel, "I Have a Wounded Faith," in *Do You Believe?* Edited by Antonio Monda and translated by Ann Goldstein. New York: Vintage Books, 2007, page 174.

57. Elie Wiesel, *Night*, page 34.

58. *AG*, page 215.

59. Ibid., page 216.

60. Elie Wiesel, *Night*, page 37.

61. Ibid., page 65.

62. *AR*, page 105.

63. Wiesel reports that Yankel Rosensaft, a Bergen-Belsen survivor, took good care of Kazin, naming him to a literary panel founded by Bergen-Belsen survivors, inviting him to various gatherings, and providing him with a luxurious hotel room, pocket money, and gifts for him and his wife. Ibid., page 336.

64. Berger, discussions with Hugh Nissenson.

65. *AR*, pages 336–337.

66. Naomi Seidman, "Elie Wiesel and the Scandal of Jewish Rage," *Jewish Social Studies Series*, 3, no. 1996, 8.

67. Margaret Myers Feinstein, "Reconsidering Jewish Rage After the Holocaust," in *The Palgrave Handbook of Holocaust Literature and Culture*. Edited by Victoria Aarons and Phyllis Lassner. Cham, Switzerland: Springer, Palgrave Macmillan, 2020, page 744. Hereafter this will be cited as "Jewish Rage."

68. Ibid., page 745.

69. Ibid., page 754. But see also Wiesel's essay "An Appointment with Hate," *Commentary*, 344, no. 6, December 1, 1962, pages 470–476.

70. "Jewish Rage," page 755.

71. Ibid.

72. Elie Wiesel, *The Fifth Son*. Translated by Marion Wiesel. New York: Summit Books, 1985, page 215.

73. Wiesel, "I Have a Wounded Faith," page 174.

74. *AG*, page 217.

75. "Jewish Rage," page 755.

76. Wiesel, "I Have a Wounded Faith," page 174.
77. *AG*, page 217.
78. *The Trial of God*. Translated by MarionWiesel. Knopf Doubleday Publishing Group. 1995, page 133.
79. Richard L. Rubenstein, "Some Perspectives on Religious Faith After Auschwitz," in *The German Church Struggle and the Holocaust*. Edited by Franklin H. Littell and Hubert G. Locke. Detroit: Wayne State University Press, 1974, page 267. Rubenstein subsequently modified his position, embracing a type of dialectical mysticism.
80. Ibid.
81. Richard L. Rubenstein, *After Auschwitz: History, Theology and Contemporary Judaism*. Second Edition. Baltimore: The Johns Hopkins University Press, 1992, page 172.
82. Ibid.
83. Ibid., pages 271–272.
84. Ibid., page 274. Wiesel reports seeing an actual Trial of God in Auschwitz presided over by three rabbis. They argued the case, both prosecuting and defending God. The verdict was rendered: guilty. One of them said, "The Court case is concluded; now it is time for the evening prayers." And they prayed. Burger, *Witness*, page 93.
85. Michael Berenbaum, *Elie Wiesel: God, the Holocaust, and the Children of Israel*. West Orange: Behrman House, Inc., 1994, pages 9–10.
86. Ibid., page 53.
87. Ibid., page 59.
88. Ibid., page 67.
89. See endnote 84.
90. Wiesel's own ambiguous position concerning the covenant is worth pondering. "I believe," he told Harry James Cargas, "during the Holocaust the covenant was broken. Maybe it will be renewed, perhaps later, maybe it was renewed even then, on a different level. So many Jews kept their faith or even strengthened it. But it was broken, because of the clouds and because of the fire." Yet he attests that he continued to pray and to believe in God—even in Auschwitz.

CHAPTER 2

ELIE WIESEL AND JEWISH-CHRISTIAN RELATIONS

A JOURNEY OF HOPE AGAINST DESPAIR

Discussing his religious life, Elie Wiesel told an interviewer that "the thirst is there, the quest is there, but the wound [the Shoah] had not been there before, and now it is." Crucially, he added, "And also my attitude toward non-Jews changed."[1] As a deeply religious child in Sighet, Wiesel recalled that he would never walk by a church, preferring to cross the street, fearful that he would be kidnapped or forcibly converted. "I was right then," he added, "but I would be wrong if I did it now."[2] Years later, reflecting on his experience in the Shoah, Wiesel was struck by what he terms a harsh truth: "In Auschwitz all the Jews were victims, all the killers were Christian."[3] Nevertheless, it is significant to note that Wiesel's attitude toward and relationship with Christianity and individual Christians evolved dramatically after the Shoah.

"It was wrong," he attested, "for Jews to ignore Christianity for two thousand years."[4] Yet, it was equally wrong for the church to embrace and disseminate antisemitism or what came to be known as the "Teaching of Contempt" for Jews and Judaism, although the magnitude of the two wrongs was radically unequal.

Authentic interfaith dialogue is, historically speaking, a new phenomenon. Ironically birthed by the Holocaust, this dialogue was initiated by two conferences, the second of which had world-wide impact. The International Emergency Conference on antisemitism was held in Seelisberg, Switzerland, in 1947. Participants included Jews, Protestants, and Catholics. Jules Isaac, the pre-eminent Jewish-French historian who lost most of his family in the Holocaust, and whose own life was saved by a Christian family who hid him, was a notable participant.

On the conference's agenda were three items: the current state of antisemitism and reasons why it continued after the Shoah; developing practical strategies for combating antisemitism; and to begin a process for healing the Jewish-Christian relationship. The conference issued the "Ten Principles" of Seelisberg, which began an attempt to deal with the Shoah's implications for Christianity.

Fifteen years later, Pope John XXIII convened the Second Vatican Council, whose task was to reassess the church's relationship to the modern world. The Italian word *aggiornamento* (updating) was used. Questions had begun to arise about the possible relationship between church teachings and the Holocaust. In essence, however, the 1965 document *Nostra Aetate* (N.A., *In Our Time*) was the most significant document issued by the council. Note four, dealing exclusively with Judaism, affirmed the theological integrity of the Jewish tradition and was nothing less than, in Professor Michael Phayer's well-chosen phrase, a "theological somersault" in which the Roman Catholic Church rejected the antisemitism which had emerged out of its 1,900 years of the Teaching of Contempt.

Subsequent implementing documents enabled far reaching changes to be instituted in church ritual and teaching. The church had, in effect, begun its move from parochialism to a more global perspective, ultimately rejecting the concept that "outside the church there is no salvation." It is significant to note that *Jubilee*, a now defunct Catholic magazine, published the first excerpts of *Night* in America. It was here that Harry James Cargas, the Catholic thinker who had many conversations with Wiesel and published two books based on these discussions; the first appeared prior to Wiesel's winning the Nobel Prize and the second afterward initially read Wiesel's memoir. It is also noteworthy that Wiesel's 1978 *Four Hasidic Masters and Their Struggle Against Melancholy*, which originated as a Ward-Phillips Lectures series at the University of Notre Dame, was published by the university press and has a Foreword written by University President Theodore M. Hesburgh, C.S.C.[5]

Interfaith in the American cultural context emerged from a complex mix of events, three outstanding among them. First, post-war America continued its embrace of religious pluralism, the embryo of which began during the Second World War and which led eventually to the founding of the National Conference of Christians and Jews (NCCJ). Second, as Professor Jonathan Sarna reminds readers, liberal-minded Protestants, Catholics and Jews worked together to promote "brotherhood." Brotherhood Day, first celebrated in 1934, 13 years later became Brotherhood Week. The work of "influential Christians and Jews . . . [pushed] Judaism from the margins of American religious life toward its very center."[6] At the same time (1948), the military became integrated under President Harry S. Truman.

America embraced religious pluralism, at least as far as Judaism and Christianity were concerned. Will Herberg's influential 1955 book *Protestant-Catholic-Jew* argued that America's religious identity was encompassed by these three religious traditions. Although there was a major demographic imbalance among the three religions, with Judaism being the smallest in number, it nevertheless was ranked as an equal component of American religious identity. In a less scholarly vein, President Dwight D. Eisenhower famously remarked: "Our form of government has no sense unless it is founded in a deeply felt religious faith, and I don't care what it is."[7] It is also significant to note that many of the American clergy who were delegates to the Second Vatican Council were theological liberals. This chapter discusses Elie Wiesel's evolving position, and impact, on Jewish-Christian dialogue. We begin first in Europe in order to better understand Wiesel's changing perception of Christianity and the importance of dialogue, as well as to comprehend more fully the distinctiveness of the American context for interfaith.

PRE-HOLOCAUST JEWISH-CHRISTIAN DIALOGUE

Christianity's Teaching of Contempt for Jews and Judaism, coupled with its triumphalist theology, rendered authentic dialogue impossible. Prior to the Shoah, "dialogue" typically consisted of the ritual humiliation of a rabbi by a priest. While it is true that individual Christians and Jews did interact, as Professor John Connelly stresses, the idea of a Jew achieving salvation was a theological impossibility for Christian believers. Business, and sometimes social, interaction was one thing, although the latter was rare. Salvation was quite a different matter. Yet in *Night*, Wiesel notes two isolated instances of Christian help for Jews in the Sighet ghetto. Maria, the family servant who spoke Yiddish and understood Jewish ritual practice, offered to hide her employers in her cabin "in a remote hamlet." Wiesel has written of her: "If other Christians had acted like her, the trains rolling toward the unknown would have been less crowded."[8] The Wiesels declined this invitation because they did not know what fate awaited them. In the second instance Wiesel's father, who served as an intercessor on behalf of the Jewish community, had a friend, an inspector in the Hungarian police, who sought to warn the family of the impending roundup of Jews. However, by the time the family had unblocked the barricaded window, the police officer had disappeared.

Wiesel also recalled two incidents from the death camps where non-Jewish prisoners said or did something to re-affirm the human image. In Auschwitz the first speech by the Polish Catholic Chief of Block 17 included the words,

> Comrades, you are now in the concentration camp Auschwitz. . . . Have faith in life, a thousand times faith. By driving out despair, you will move away from death. Hell does not last forever. . . . And now, here is a prayer, or rather a piece of advice: let there be camaraderie among you. We are all brothers and share the same fate.

Wiesel concludes this passage by writing, "Those were the first human words."[9]

In Buchenwald, the final camp in which Wiesel was imprisoned and where his father perished, the chief of his block, a non-Jewish Czech, saved the entire block of a few hundred children. These two acts of altruism imprinted themselves on the teenager's consciousness. "These people," Wiesel writes, "stand out."

WIESEL'S STANCE ON INTERFAITH DIALOGUE: SHIFTING PERSPECTIVE

Wiesel, as noted, was a God-intoxicated youth in Sighet. His life revolved around the teachings and rituals of Judaism which provided him a sacred canopy under whose shelter he lived. He remembers Moishe the Beadle, his teacher, asking, Why do you pray? Wiesel mused, "Why did I pray? Strange question. Why did I live? Why did I breathe?"[10] Moreover, he reported that during the early years of the war he was absorbed in his Jewish studies. He told the Catholic scholar Harry James Cargas, "I was more aware about what went on three thousand years ago than what was going on in the present."[11] Christianity evoked neither his interest nor curiosity. Quite to the contrary; the Christian faith appeared totally Other, and antithetical to his own. He was unaware that Judaism birthed Christianity, nor that the two traditions claimed certain similar traditions and teachings. His visceral fear of Christianity was so great that as a child he avoided walking by a church lest he would be physically harmed and/or forced to convert. Significantly, Wiesel writes: "It is only when I reached adulthood that I understood the importance of dialogue between people of different religions. I understood the danger of living in a world made of stereotypes."[12] I shall return to this point shortly.

Wiesel viewed the Holocaust as a paradigm shattering event that demands both a rethinking of Enlightenment certainties and the notion of a covenant. Was the covenant at Sinai broken in Auschwitz? At certain moments Wiesel said yes. However, he also said it was renewed.[13] The

Nobel laureate writes that "at Auschwitz not only man died, but also the idea of man. . . . It was its own heart the world incinerated at Auschwitz."[14] Wiesel emphatically noted that the first impact of his iconic memoir *Night* was on Catholic and Protestant intellectuals who "felt that a tremendous confession of guilt was necessary." As an aside, Wiesel also commented on the irony engendered by the fact that it was only after his books and message had been accepted by certain Christian thinkers that the Jewish community began reading his work. This perhaps reflects the feeling of vulnerability and defensiveness that many in the American Jewish community felt in the aftermath of the Holocaust. This was also at a time when interfaith dialogue was only beginning to emerge as a viable path to travel.

When Wiesel arrived in America in 1955 he found a complex inter-religious landscape. On the one hand, traces of the foul odor of antisemitism which had peaked during the Second World War still lingered in the air. We have already noted the "unholy trinity" of antisemitic cultural icons: Charles Lindbergh ("Lucky Lindy"), Henry Ford, and Father Charles E. Coughlin in the 1920s and 1930s. Others, such as the syndicated columnist Westbrook Pegler, added to the growth of antisemitism before the war.

But when the war began Lindbergh and Coughlin were in disgrace for their pro-Nazi speeches. By 1942 "Lucky" Lindbergh had been stripped of his commission in the Army and probably avoided being investigated and prosecuted only because of his great fame. The government nearly prosecuted Father Coughlin for sedition, but this was averted when Coughlin's bishop forbade him from any public activities in 1942. By then he was already much diminished as most radio stations would no longer air his hate-filled programs. That year Ford apologized for his previous antisemitic activities in a letter to the Anti-Defamation League (ADL), the leading Jewish civil rights organization in the country. Ford spent considerable money to suppress one of his own publications, *The International Jew*, although personally he remained a classic antisemitic bigot. In the 1940s and 1950s Pegler, the widely read columnist, endorsed their antisemitic views in appealing to America's nativistic and xenophobic cultural strains. During the war the Justice Department considered charging him with sedition. In 1962 he was fired from his newspaper position and disappeared from general public view. Other antisemites wrote and spoke in this period, although increasingly they were marginalized by political leaders in both major political parties. Although by the time Wiesel came to the U.S. Coughlin had been shut down for more than a dozen years, Lindbergh no longer spouted his antisemitic nonsense, Ford was dead, and Pegler was almost finished as well, many people were influenced by these and other openly antisemitic figures.

Nineteen hundred years of the Teaching of Contempt were not easily discarded, but by the 1960s, in part because of reactions to the Shoah and the trial of Adolph Eichmann in 1961, antisemitism was clearly less virulent than it had been before World War II. Illustrative of this emphatic exposure of cultural antisemitism is the popular movie *Gentleman's Agreement*, which was nominated for eight Academy Awards in 1947. It won three, including best picture of the year.

As historian Jonathan Sarna writes: "In response to wartime antisemitism, liberal Jews and Christians joined together to promote 'better understanding' and 'goodwill.'"[15] The National Conference of Christians and Jews worked to help create a "new and more religiously pluralistic image of America." Interfaith became immortalized in a manner of speaking when in 1948 an American postage stamp was issued commemorating the heroism of four chaplains, two Protestants, a Catholic, and a Jew, who had given their life vests to seaman aboard the ill-fated USS *Dorchester*, torpedoed in 1943. The four chaplains, in a selfless act of altruism, "arm in arm in prayer," went down with the ship.[16] Interfaith dialogue was in its infancy but began to gain new currency for a variety of reasons, including the growing liberalism of American democracy and an emerging post-war commitment to human rights.

Mention should also be made of *Nostra Aetate*'s (hereafter referred to as N.A.) liberalizing impact on American culture. The American bishops who attended the Second Vatican Council were, on the whole, liberal and endorsed N.A. It should also be remembered that the drive for improving Jewish-Christian relations and the proclamation of National Brotherhood Week were very much a part of mainstream American culture. N.A. was a major point of departure for Catholic religious thought. The proclamation noted that religions other than Catholicism had their own validity, but its most significant statement in this regard was note four, with its reversal of the church's long history of antisemitism, thereby opening the door to a positive evaluation of Jewish theology and, consequently, improved relations with Judaism as well as other traditions. Wiesel's message of the possibility of authentic interfaith dialogue was viewed as a step in the right ecumenical direction.

But Wiesel himself first had to work through his own traumatic Holocaust legacy. In addition to his memoir, his first two novels, *Dawn* and *The Accident* (*Le Jour, Day*)—in the French original—portray, in the words of Professor Ellen Fine, "the voyage away from his origins, the long descent into the multiple layers of darkness that dispossessed him of his identity, his traditions, his community."[17] At that particular moment, Wiesel was wrestling like the biblical Jacob with the monumental task of seeking to reconcile the beliefs of the God-intoxicated youth he had been and the post-Shoah theologically traumatized Holocaust survivor that he had become. During the time that Wiesel's three books were written (1955–1960), one of the most popular plays on Broadway was *The Diary of Anne Frank*, directed by Garson Kanin and revised by playwrights Frances Goodrich and Albert Hackett. The play presented a sanitized version of the Holocaust, intentionally omitting Anne's more fearful observations. The playwrights essentially Christianized the diary, evidently with the consent of Anne's father, Otto Frank. Focusing on the optimistic passages in Anne's diary, they stressed Anne's observation: "In spite of everything I believe in the goodness of people." Omitted was Anne's more ominous and accurate statement: "I hear the approaching thunder which will destroy us all." As historian Deborah E. Lipstadt writes: "Uplift and optimism were in the American air. This production of the diary provided more of it."[18] It is instructive at this point to emphasize that Wiesel observed on more than one occasion that his Holocaust experience began where Anne's ended.

In what follows I discuss Wiesel's post-Shoah interfaith dialogues, initially in Europe and then in America, and elsewhere note his increasing engagement with Christianity. I also discuss two of Wiesel's novels that illustrate and illuminate both his evolving position on interfaith dialogue and his understanding of the relationship between Jewish particularity and the universality of his message. Wiesel forthrightly asserted his starting point for engaging in interfaith dialogue. "I am a Jew," he writes, "and I try out of my Jewishness to help other people understand my religion and their own."[19] This declaration, in turn, leads to the essential historical and theological questions for Jewish-Christian dialogue. He asked, "Can one erase two-thousand years of suspicion and persecution endured under the shadow of the cross?" The answer is no, one cannot; nor should one. "Only if we forget nothing," he attested, "shall we succeed in abolishing what divides us."[20] Authentic dialogue, therefore, requires both memory of the past and hope for the future.

WHAT DIVIDES CHRISTIANS AND JEWS?

The fundamental divide between Judaism and Christianity is the issue of the Messiah. Christianity awaits the Messiah's Second Coming, and Judaism speaks of his/her first appearance on earth. Eschewing the question of the Messiah's identity, one must first define his/her function. In addition to ushering in an era of world peace, the function of the Messiah is to unite people. Consequently, attested Wiesel, "A Messiah that divides the Jewish people is a false Messiah."[21] Wiesel further observed, "Jesus more than anyone else in history, provoked dissension and division in the world. So many massacres were conducted in his name. Can that be the Messiah?"[22] Moreover, he points to misinterpretations, willful or otherwise, of religion which occur when followers misinterpret the message of the founder. "As far as the Jews are concerned," Wiesel told Cargas that Jesus "may be retroactively guilty for all the murders and massacres that were done in his name. I believe that the Christians betrayed the Christ more than the Jews did."[23] In discussion Wiesel told me "that problems occur when men claim to act in God's name or, even worse, when they claim to be God."[24]

Wiesel's novels reveal the ugliness of the "longest hatred," which reached its apogee in the unprecedented spasm of murder and horror unleashed during the Holocaust and whose violent legacy in terms of preventable deaths and disregard of the sanctity of human life continues to plague the earth in the era of the COVID-19 pandemic. Yet, these novels simultaneously provide glimpses of the isolated few Christians who sought to help their Jewish brothers and sisters during the time of testing. These antipathies do not, of course, cancel one another. They do, however, compel one to ponder the mystery of goodness which, for Wiesel, exceeded that of evil. Moreover, the acts of the righteous gentiles demonstrate that humans always have a choice between good and evil, between listening to their conscience and abandoning all moral considerations.

The present offers more than a glimmer of hope, despite the continuing spread of antisemitic propaganda and outright calumny against Judaism. The provocative and distorted film *The Passion of the Christ* made by Mel Gibson, a Catholic who rejects the teachings of Vatican II and denies legitimacy to all popes who succeeded Pius XII, the wartime pope, is the most egregious example. Wiesel told me that this film was "the Second Crucifixion of Jesus and clearly anti-Semitic."[25] "But," Wiesel also told me in an interview, "never have Jewish-Christian relations been as good as they are now."[26] He called Pope John XXIII the "great man in Christianity, [who] was the first to open the church, to admit its failings, and to correct the liturgy omitting all the insulting sentences."[27] Elie thought John XXIII was a saint. Saints can in fact have a sense of humor. A Jewish delegation visited the pope in the Vatican and asked how many people worked there. John XXIII thought for a moment and said, "about half." Wiesel, responding to this anecdote, said "and the question is, which half?"[28] He also engaged in important dialogues with Cardinals John O'Connor and Jean-Marie Lustiger and Professor Johann Baptist Metz. Moreover, he dialogued as well with the Dalai Lama, who inquired to the secret of how the Jewish people stayed together during their long diaspora.

Wiesel's influence on Christian thought is profound, and is especially pronounced in the work of several influential American religious thinkers: Mary Boys (a prominent Catholic voice in the Jewish-Christian dialogue),

Robert McAfee Brown (a distinguished Protestant theologian), Harry James Cargas (Catholic interpreter of Wiesel's work), Alice and Roy Eckardt (Protestant theologians), Franklin H. Littell (noted as the grandfather of Holocaust Studies in America), Fa. John Pawlikowski (Catholic theologian and prolific writer on Catholic-Jewish relations), Sister Carol Rittner (Catholic theologian and first director of The Elie Wiesel Foundation for Humanity), John K. Roth (Protestant thinker, theologian, and winner of the National Professor of the Year award, Carnegie Foundation for the Advancement of Teaching, 1988), and Paul Van Buren (a Catholic who headed the Department of Religion at Temple University), among others. In return, these thinkers felt compelled by Wiesel's message to re-examine their own traditions' teachings about Jews. Moreover, various American religious institutions and agencies in dialogue with Wiesel's work sought their own *Hesbon haNefesh* (reckoning of the soul). Influential non-Jewish thinkers and lay people attended Wiesel's public lectures. Many thousands of college and university students were influenced—and challenged by—his campus presentations.

Perhaps most significantly, as we have noted, he owed much to François Mauriac, the great French Catholic writer and Nobel Laureate in Literature who personally took Wiesel's *Night* manuscript to various publishers. Although Wiesel's past was seared by the flames of the Shoah, he remained open to dialogue. He was first and foremost a witness committed to memory. Yedidyah, (beloved of God) a character in Wiesel's 2010 novel *The Sonderberg Case*, emphasizes the author's relationship to his Holocaust past: "We don't live in the past," the protagonist states, "but the past lives in us."[29] It is this attestation which imbued Wiesel with a sense of mission to bear witness to the living on behalf of the Shoah's victims. Moreover, America's commitment to memory was, in Wiesel's estimation, an ennobling characteristic of the country.

PRE-HOLOCAUST INTERFAITH RELATIONS

Prior to the Holocaust there was no serious interfaith effort. Christian theologians and thinkers rarely granted Jews either theological autonomy or validation. From the perspective of most Christian religious leaders, pre-Holocaust interfaith meant that Jews must agree that Christianity is superior. The Jewish and Christian communities distrusted one another. Christianity was viewed as an oppressor religion. As Professor Richard Rubenstein notes, they found themselves in a position of "disconfirming otherness"; for one to be true the other, by definition, had to be false. Pogroms—state sanctioned violence against Jews—were typically the only organized interaction Christianity had with Judaism. However, in Western

Europe there were also acts of violence against Jews. For example, the trial of Alfred Dreyfus in France was nothing short of an antisemitic show trial. The much-vaunted French Revolutionary slogan "Liberty, Equality, and Fraternity" was greatly resisted by three prominent groups in French society: the aristocracy, the Catholic Church, and the military. It is true that liberal impulses were present in Western Europe: the Balfour Declaration, Protestant support for Zionism, and in the United States a strong desire to bring Jewish voters into American political parties. By 1955, when Wiesel arrived in America, there had been three Jewish Supreme Court Justices, many Jews in the House of Representatives, and some in the Senate and in presidential cabinets.

As a deeply religious child in Sighet, Wiesel was heir to the inheritance of periodic acts of violence perpetrated by the Christian community against Jews. He would cross the street rather than walk by a church where, according to the teachings of his community, great danger lurked. He had no knowledge that "Judaism and Christianity claimed the same roots." At this stage of his life Wiesel, for good reason, was incapable of even conceiving of a dialogical relationship with Christianity. "Though our universes existed side by side," he wrote, "I avoided penetrating theirs, whereas they sought to dominate ours by force."[30]

Post-Shoah: Affirming Jewish Faith, Exploring Dialogue

Two novels which appeared two years apart (1964, 1966), *The Town Beyond the Wall*, divided into four prayers rather than chapters, and *The Gates of the Forest*, divided into four seasons, initiate Wiesel's search for a *tikkun* (repair) of both the self (*tikkun atzmi*) and the world (*tikkun ha-olam*). On the one hand, he seeks to affirm the Jewish tradition after the Holocaust, even while attesting that his faith has been wounded. On the other hand, he begins to explore the possibility of authentic Jewish-Christian dialogue. It is important to understand that for Wiesel, authentic dialogue always included God, especially according to the teachings of the Hasidic tradition, which was a fundamental part of his identity. When a person speaks, contended Wiesel, three voices are heard: a person speaks to God; God is by definition everywhere; therefore, by definition, God is *in* the person who listens and in the person who speaks; and the voice of God, which is the voice of His silence or the voice of the infinite.[31] Furthermore, these two novels initiate their author's commitment to life affirmation, to the importance of friendship, and to social action.

Michael ("who is like God"), the protagonist of *The Town Beyond the Wall*, returns to his hometown (*Szerencseváros*, city of luck) after the war, where he confronts and indicts the apathy of the Christian onlookers/ bystanders who passively watched as their Jewish neighbors were rounded up. This led Wiesel to observe that "the opposite of love is not hate. The opposite of love is indifference." Observed by an anonymous face peering from a window, Michael is turned over to the communist authorities, who arrest and torture him. The torturers have diabolically termed torture "prayer," forcing the prisoner to stand while he/she prayed until their knees gave out.

As the novel unfolds, the protagonist saves two lives. Menachem ("comforter"), who is described as having the moving face "of a Byzantine Christ," is almost strangled by a demented young prisoner. Michael intercedes and saves him.

Pedro, a non-Jew, is Michael's friend who enabled him to enter Hungary illegally. Despite being tortured, Michael refuses to disclose information about Pedro, thus saving his life. Significantly, as Professor Frederick Downing observes, "Wiesel has transformed the divine human dialogue into a program of solidarity with the needy, the oppressed, and the unfortunate children of God."[32] Furthermore, Pedro, who is Mexican and has memories not of the Shoah but of the Spanish Civil War, cautions Michael: "He who thinks about God, forgetting man, runs the risk of mistaking his goal: God may be your next-door neighbor." Pedro is proud of Michael for saving Menachem's life. Through a dream-like sequence he tells Michael that next he must cure the would-be strangler: "Cure him. He'll save you," attests Pedro. Michael looks into the face of the mute prisoner and thereby symbolically reaches out to humanity. Pedro recites a personal prayer made just for him. "Oh God, give me the strength to sin against you, to oppose your will! Give me the strength to Deny you, reject you, imprison you, ridicule you!" Michael endorses this antinomian prayer as it does not absolve God of Holocaust guilt.

Dialogue with humanity, notes Robert McAfee Brown, "turns out to be a dialogue between humanity and God as well." Echoing Martin Buber's position, "God is present at any point of meeting between two who reach out toward one another," Wiesel's view has obvious importance for Jewish-Christian dialogue as well. In addition, *The Town Beyond the Wall* is the first of Wiesel's books that is life-affirming and provides the initial impetus for what would become his life of passion for social justice.

Wiesel's earliest sustained literary treatment of Christianity occurs in *The Gates of the Forest*, a novel which is set both in Europe and America. He described this novel as both a "song of remembrance for Maria," who was the family housekeeper in Sighet, and as a "flight from myself into myself."[33] It is significant that Wiesel's novels, unlike his public lectures, focus much more on Christian animosity to Judaism. This volume is the author's dialogue with Menachem Mendel Schneerson, the Lubavitcher Rebbe, concerning the relationship of God to the Shoah. The encounter took place in Brooklyn at the Lubavitch court (headquarters) during a *fahrbrengen* (Hasidic study gathering).

Gavriel ("man of God" in Hebrew) and Gregor had exchanged names in the beginning of the novel in order to save Gavriel's life. Gregor asks Rebbe Schneerson how he can still believe in God after the Shoah. Unbowed, the Rebbe asks, "How can you *not* believe in God after what has happened?" The holy man admits that God is guilty of being an "ally of evil, of death, of murder."[34] However, he continues, "Who says that power comes from a shout, an outcry rather than from a prayer? The man who goes singing to his death is the brother of the man who goes to death fighting."[35] Reflecting on this encounter, Wiesel contended that he accepted the Rebbe's response not as an answer but as one more question. See *All Rivers Run to the Sea page 403*. *The Gates of the Forest* deepens and enriches Wiesel's view of the deity as he struggles to reconcile his pre-Holocaust beliefs with the horror of his Holocaust experience. From this point on, Wiesel committed himself to the fight for social justice on behalf of all who are oppressed, as I set out in Chapter 5.

The "Teaching of Contempt"
Gavriel is a Hungarian Jew in hiding but visible, the alleged illegitimate son of Maria's sister Ileana—a reputed prostitute. In addition to his checkered birth, he is presented to the villagers as a deaf mute. Consequently, they view him as a safe repository for their secrets, which include affairs with Ileana. Moreover, the local priest in the confessional booth—where he sits as the penitent—reveals that he had betrayed a Jew seeking refuge from forced conversion. The priest personifies the Christian tradition and its betrayal both of Jews and the Jewish people which rested on the fatal implications resulting from the church's two-millenia teaching of contempt.

The town stages a passion play where Gregor is cast as Judas. The tension mounts as the performers on stage begin to avenge the death of their master by punishing Judas. Hurling epithets at Gregor/Judas encourages the audience. Initially, they shout support for the actors. Then they surge onto the stage and begin to beat "Judas." Bloodied, Gregor begins to shout. Judas is the only one who can forgive the villages' sinners. Judas and not Jesus is the victim. The "injustice toward Judas," notes Robert McAfee Brown, "is being replicated six million times . . . two thousand years of victimizing members of the race of Judas (and Jesus)."[36] Judas is the prototypical traitor in Passion Plays.

Wiesel employed the infamous Oberammergau Passion Play (a passion play is a religious drama, medieval in origin, which portrays the suffering, death, and resurrection of Jesus Christ) as a literary trope for a decisive scene which takes place in Eastern Europe and which encapsulates the pre-Shoah attitudes of both Christianity and Judaism toward one another. The task of passion plays was to re-enforce negative and hostile attitudes towards Jews and Judaism, the more hatred of the Jewish tradition, the more "successful" the play. On the one hand there is Christian hostility toward Jews and Judaism. On the other hand, Wiesel "wished to say certain things about our attitude toward Christianity."[37] Originating in the Bavarian village of Oberammergau, the play—performed every ten years since 1634—portrays the primal animus of traditional Christianity toward Judaism based on the Gospel accounts of the passion and resurrection of Jesus. The villagers of Oberammergau had vowed to God that they would perform a passion play if they were spared the effects of the Bubonic Plague (seventeenth century). Thoroughly antisemitic in tone and character, the performance vilifies Jews as a deicide people and Judas as the betrayer of Jesus. It also puts the blame for his death solely on Jewish shoulders. Historically, the passion play served to harden Christianity's heart against Jews and Judaism, reinforcing negative Christian stereotypes concerning the Jewish tradition.

It is significant to note a positive development over the last 30 years in the presentation of the Oberammergau performances. Hitler viewed the play in 1934 and praised it for its portrayal of the menace of world Jewry. But the Second Vatican Council in N.A. rejected the claim of collective Jewish guilt in the death of Jesus. Change began in 1987 when Christian Stucki was chosen to direct the play. He introduced the notion of a Jewish Jesus. Moreover, both the American Jewish Committee (AJC) and the Inter-Defamation League (ADL) have sent representatives from their offices of interreligious affairs committees to work with the presenters of this play. Stucki continues as the play's director. The result has been a toning down of the performance's hardcore antisemitism. In addition, the AJC formed an academic advisory group that consults with Stucki in addressing the play's continuing antisemitic bias.

The passion play is, attests Professor Victoria Aarons, "a play within a play."[38] It portrays the death of the Jewish Messiah for Christians but not for Jews. Jesus has been Christianized and thereby transformed into the Christian savior (son of God). This accounts for the eternality of Christian antisemitism And the acting out of a tradition of revenge. In addition, He is unsparing in his description of the sheer indifference of those perpetrating this crime. Wiesel achieves his purposes by juxtaposing historical events with scenes from the play. He writes in part two of the novel:

Officers in dazzling uniforms stood in front of the firing squads, raising their arms and calling out, "Fire, fire, fire!" And soldiers bored, fired their machine guns, indifferent, thinking of nothing, not even of death. And hundreds of hearts ceased beating, ceased advancing toward a future at the end of which a Messiah—it didn't matter who—was supposed to receive them. "Fire!" called out the officers, and the Messiah himself, a thousand times, a thousand, thousand times multiplied, fell into the ditch.[39]

This calls to mind images of Wehrmacht troops seated on the edge of a pit, smoking cigarettes and firing their machine guns at the Jews who, naked and forsaken, crowded into the pit. As "the executioners were moving closer to the stage . . . Gregor did not flinch," writes Wiesel:

At the very same moment, in the crimson fields of Galicia, smartly turned-out officers were shouting the order: "Fire! Fire!" A hundred Jews, ten thousand Jews were tumbling into the ditches. He would not die alone. . . . All Jews in Nazi dominated Europe shared a similar fate or would have had the Allied victory not ended the Holocaust.[40]

In his 2005 novel *The Time of the Uprooted*, Wiesel again reveals the fact that during the Shoah many Christians were in fact guilty of apostasy. The fictional Catholic Archbishop Baranyi gives Hananel ("merciful God"), a rebbe, a choice: convert or die. Hananel replies, "With every Jew you kill, you put your Lord back on the cross."[41]

Tell me, man of the Church, do you know what you are doing to your Lord when you allow these murderers to massacre the descendants of Abraham, Isaac, and Jacob? And you dare to speak of saving my soul when it is your own that is in perdition?[42]

CHRISTIANS WHO HELPED JEWS

Gregor/Gavriel, the *The Gates of the Forest* protagonist, is a Hungarian Jew hidden by Maria, the now aging former servant of the Wiesels, who first appeared in *Night*. She had been with the family for many years and spoke excellent Yiddish. Parenthetically, as noted earlier, there is also a tribute to Maria in volume one (*All Rivers Run to the Sea*) of Elie's memoirs. Maria offered to hide the entire family in her secluded mountain cabin. "Dear Maria," writes Wiesel, "if other Christians had acted like her, the trains rolling toward the unknown would have been less crowded."[43] As we have also mentioned, a nameless police detective in *Night* sought unsuccessfully to warn the Wiesel family of the impending Nazi roundup of Jews. Wiesel discovered this fact years later.

"And yet," in this novel—as previously noted—there is recognition of the saving deed of Ilona, a Christian cabaret singer who risks her life to save Gamliel Friedman, whom she hid for several years. Gamliel, unlike Gregor, is in hiding and hidden.

Seeds of Dialogue

Wiesel, while portraying the murderous antisemitic rage of the villagers, does recognize the few *Hasidei Umot HaOlam* (Righteous Among the Nations) who act to save Jewish life. In addition to Maria—Wiesel terms the novel "a song of remembrance for Maria," a mysterious and only partially sketched figure—Petruskanu, the village's mayor, rescues Gregor, taking him in his carriage to the forest where he rendezvous with partisans. Wiesel alludes to the fact that the mayor may have been Ileana's lover. Furthermore, in this novel Wiesel broadens our understanding of the Messiah in having Gregor tell Clara, his wife, "The Messiah isn't one man . . . he's all men. As long as there are men there will be a Messiah." Wiesel here shifts the main responsibility for maintaining the covenant from God to the human partner. How humans behave toward one another is a gauge of how close, or far away, the Messiah is.

Good Versus Evil: The Eternal Struggle

Wiesel's more recent novel, *The Judges*, set in America, involves a battle between the forces of evil and good. The judge, a non-Jew, assumes the role of God in the lives of his five prisoners who had survived a plane crash. Although a judge is not in charge of prisoners but supervises the trial, in Wiesel's novel the judge is judge, jury, and executioner. Wiesel sketches psychologically acute portraits of each of the protagonists as they muse on their impending doom. In Carole J. Lambert's intelligent reading of the novel, she opines that "Wiesel may be suggesting that the God Whom he has interrogated since the Shoah has a dark, evil side."[44] The fact that the judge is either murdered or compelled to commit suicide by his deformed servant before carrying out his judicially intended murders deepens the mystery of this figure. In Wiesel's literary rendition the judge exceeds his moral function in seeking to murder his prisoners. The novel indicates that the forces of evil succumb—eventually—to those of good. Wiesel's literary victory over evil is, however, far from being replicated in reality. Combating the evil of antisemitism is the millennial task lying before the Christian-Jewish dialogue as each tradition engages in the eternal task of messianic waiting.

As this eternal task of messianic waiting unfolds in its own inexorable time, it is heartening to note the existence of some positive developments, which have occurred on both the institutional and personal levels.

Professional organizations such as the American Jewish Committee and the Anti-Defamation League have found willing dialogue partners in many parts of the Vatican. Moreover, there are an increasing number of college and university courses on interfaith relations. These are all promising signs. We turn now to the issue of personal encounters.

PERSONAL ENCOUNTERS

FRANÇOIS MAURIAC

In 1954 Elie Wiesel met with François Mauriac, the great Catholic writer and winner of the 1952 Nobel Prize in Literature. This was his first important post-Shoah intellectual encounter with a non-Nazi Christian. Concerning other Christian intellectual's in post-war Paris,Wiesel did not study with Jean-Paul Sartre, but was familiar with his writings. A similar situation existed between Wiesel and the novelists Albert Camus and Andre Malraux. Wiesel met Mauriac at a reception arranged by a friend of his. The young writer himself arranged to meet Mauriac. This meeting was in fact a turning point in Wiesel's life, launching his career as a writer and compelling him to articulate the essential difference between Judaism and Christianity concerning the figure of Jesus and the role of suffering in human life. Wiesel writes: "The fact is that, practically, I owe François Mauriac my career. He was a Christian and we were very close. Had it not been for Mauriac, I would have become or remained an obscure writer, a journalist."[45] Wiesel went to Mauriac's apartment, ostensibly to seek the great writer's help in arranging an interview with Pierre Mendes France, the country's Jewish prime minister. The French writer began discussing the greatness of Jesus who, as the son of God, was unable to save Israel but did save the world. This angered Wiesel. As Frederick Downing writes: "Perhaps he was angered by Mauriac's praise of human suffering against his own memories of the atrocities of the camps, or perhaps it was the memory of his own childhood and the anti-Semitism of Christians."[46]

> At that moment of truth, I chose to personify the Jewish avenger, while he, this Christian writer because of his fame and; "piled up with honors" incarnated for me the whole Christian world, from its origins to our own days, its history and its path, its kings and its priests that based their faith on the death of a Jew, on the death of all Jews. I was going to shout: do not cry, it's too late, all the tears of all the Christians will not be able to erase the spilled blood.[47]

Wiesel's meeting with Mauriac crystalized many things for the young writer. Theologically, Jesus as the Christ was a "stumbling block" for Judaism and a "cornerstone" for Christianity. But as Shlomo the seer exclaims to the crucified Jesus in *A Beggar in Jerusalem*, it is the Jews who will "suffer for (Jesus) because of (Jesus)." The older French author wrote a Foreword to *Night*, which has appeared in every edition since. Cargas, who referred to himself as a post-Auschwitz Catholic and later wrote two books of conversations with Wiesel, contends that this Foreword "may be seen as a personal encyclical from a Christian to a Jew."[48] Furthermore, Mauriac dedicated his book *The Son of Man* to Wiesel, terming him a "crucified Jewish child who stands for many others." Mauriac for his part was no blind ideologue. As Wiesel noted, the French author was one of the first to denounce Pope Pius XII's silence. Wiesel accepted the gift of Mauriac's book but told him "the comparison with Jesus Christ is surely not applicable to me because of my background, because of my attitude, and because of my belief."[49]

The two writers remained friends even though they had their theological differences. Wiesel shared vignettes of discussions the two writers had. How do humans testify for God? "Christians," writes Wiesel, "say through suffering. We say, through faith."[50] Intensifying the difference in the two traditions' view of Jesus, Wiesel told Mauriac that "the Nazi killers and torturers were baptized." Mauriac defended Jesus, contending, "It is not His fault if we betray His love for us." Wiesel responded, "I'm not blaming Jesus. He was crucified by the Romans and now it is the Christians who torment him by committing evil in his name."[51] These disputations were an essential feature of their relationship and underscore Wiesel's insistence on authenticity and honesty in any meaningful dialogue. Wiesel promised to write a book about their disputations. It was to be called *Disputations*. If such a manuscript is discovered, it will further enrich our understanding of the two writers' relationship as well as shed further light on Wiesel's understanding of Jewish-Christian encounter.

CARDINAL JEAN-MARIE LUSTIGER

Wiesel's dialogue with the then Archbishop of Paris Jean-Marie Lustiger reveals an entirely different tone than his interaction with Mauriac. In the first place, the archbishop, born a Jew (his name is Aaron), converted during the Shoah in which his mother perished. Lustiger does not hide his Jewish roots; indeed, he delights in speaking Yiddish, but makes the troubling claim of being a "fulfilled Jew."[52] It is alleged that Israel Meir Lau, then Chief Ahkenazi Rabbi of the country, refused to meet with Lustiger because he had failed to re-embrace his Jewish identity. Be that as it may, Wiesel's dialogue with Lustiger was both a Jewish-Jewish encounter— again reminiscent of Shlomo and Jesus in *A Beggar in Jerusalem*—and a Jewish-Christian interface. Wiesel wondered if Lustiger, "a Jew turned Christian is 'fulfilled,' does this mean he is a better Jew than those who have remained Jewish?" This thought prompted Wiesel to reflect on the centuries of conflict between Christianity and Judaism, beginning with the "hateful writings" of the church fathers and including the official silence of Pius XII during—and after—the Shoah. Prior to their meeting, Wiesel weighed two conflicting admonitions. His Talmudic master, Saul Lieberman, resolved never to shake the hand of a *meshumad* (renegade). The Talmud, however, states: "A Jew, even a sinner, remains a Jew." The question is: "How is one to classify Aaron Lustiger?" Crucially distinguishing between the past and the present, "Today's Christian," writes Wiesel, "is not responsible for what his ancestors did long ago."[53]

Wiesel approached his meeting with Lustiger with one basic question: can one be Jewish and Christian at the same time? Wiesel believed "a synergy of religions is both possible and necessary, but only in total honesty." He wished to convert no one and wanted no one to convert him. The two men conversed for a long time. One positive result of their dialogue was that Lustiger stopped using the term "fulfilled Jew." Moreover, he continued defending Jewish causes and the State of Israel. The two continued their dialogue long after their initial meeting. Wiesel referred to him as a friend and was certain their friendship would endure. They often consulted each other when problems arose on matters of Jewish-Christian relations. But as far as Wiesel's question concerning the possibility of being both Jewish and Christian simultaneously, this query remained unanswered, and is perhaps unanswerable. Moreover, unlike his declared intention to publish a book about his relationship with François Mauriac, Wiesel stated that much of his dialogue with Lustiger would remain confidential.

THE AMERICAN CONTEXT

Turning to America, Wiesel found many more dialogue partners who were deeply influenced by his witness bearing and its impact on their relationship to Christianity and to interfaith dialogue. This is in part due, as noted earlier, to America's commitment to religious pluralism. It also has much to do with the wall of separation between church and state (as Thomas Jefferson put it) in this country as opposed to the European model. This is not to ignore the fact that anti-Jewish attitudes and actions persisted in America. To cite but one example, the Church of Latter-Day Saints (Mormons) took up the abhorrent practice of baptizing the souls of Jews murdered in the Holocaust. This activity persisted despite a pledge by the Mormon leadership to stop. At one point during the 2012 presidential campaign, Wiesel wrote to Mitt Romney, the Republican presidential candidate and a member of the Mormon Church, seeking his assistance in stopping this posthumous baptizing. The names of Wiesel, his father, and his grandfather had been entered into a database for possible baptism.

Nearly two decades ago Wiesel was asked to comment on the state of Catholic-Jewish relations in this country. In a dialogue with Cardinal O'Connor, Wiesel mentioned that there are "ups and downs." But that when he met with the Cardinal he felt "we are making headway. We are," he continued, "open and honest."[54] Wiesel spoke out of his Jewishness in order to help others understand his religion and their own. He had total respect for the cardinal as a Christian. Commenting on the two different— Catholic and Jewish—approaches to seeking converts, "Jews," Wiesel attested, "never believed that it was our duty to turn the whole world Jewish. Our mission was to make the world more hospitable."[55]

Despite, or rather because of, his commitment to honest interfaith dialogue, Wiesel did not hesitate to call out continuing instances of Christian antisemitism as exemplified by the aforementioned Gibson film and the Holocaust-denying Bishop Richard Williamson.

Bishop Williamson is a member of the Society of St Pius the X, which is a traditionalist branch of Catholicism. He is a British citizen who has been excommunicated twice. The church, I believe, mistakenly assumed that this antisemite would somehow reform himself. He was also excommunicated in Germany for denying the Holocaust. The church stirred a theological hornets' nest when Pope Benedict XVI readmitted Williamson to membership without the disgraced clergyman offering any expression of regret. Evidently, a desire for ecclesiological unity overcame common sense in this unfortunate event.

Furthermore, the early actions of Pope John Paul II also raised a red flag. He failed to mention the word J-E-W in his 1979 Auschwitz homily. He subsequently welcomed the antisemitic Kurt Waldheim, a Nazi officer during the Holocaust, on a state visit to the Vatican, where the pope unbelievably described him as a man "devoted to securing peace among people."[56] In 1998 Elie Wiesel responded to the ugliness surrounding the dispute over the crosses planted at Auschwitz. Noting the profound differences concerning the symbolism of the cross: "compassion, love, and mercy for the Christian . . . a symbol of persecution for the Jew," it is, he opined, best "not to have any religious symbol [in Auschwitz]."[57] Teresa Świeboka of the Auschwitz museum falsely criticized Wiesel's position, claiming it was based on the fact that he did not believe in God. Wiesel later told me in response that his view was in fact based on the fact that *he does believe in God.*[58]

In America, Wiesel befriended many religious leaders, including the Dalai Lama, who sought his counsel on the secret of how the Jewish people maintained their identity during their long exile from the land of Israel. As the impact of N.A. gradually increased, many interfaith dialogue groups emerged on the American scene. Various Jewish agencies, including the American Jewish Committee and the Anti-Defamation League, had special departments devoted to dialoging with Christian partners. Among the many American Christian scholars with whom Wiesel interacted and whose views of Judaism and Christianity were profoundly affected, I make reference to the following: Sister Mary Boys, Robert McAfee Brown, Harry James Cargas, Franklin H. Littell, Fa. John Pawlikowski, Sister Carol Rittner, and John K. Roth. Collectively, these thinkers did much to educate their respective faith communities about the need for self-critiquing their own tradition and for broadening their understanding of Judaism.

Sister Mary Boys

Mary Boys is a prominent Catholic scholar in the field of religious education focusing especially on Jewish-Christian dialogue. Growing up in Seattle just prior to the liberal era of the Second Vatican Council had a significant influence on her determination to "learn in the presence of the other," while seeking to dispel the hateful and harmful stereotypes of "the Jews" found in the Christian Scriptures and in the writings of the church fathers. Professor Boys and Dr. Sara Lee collaborated in writing an important scholarly volume on Christian-Jewish learning and dialogue. This volume stresses the significance of fully listening to and learning from the religious Other. Boys is the Skinner and McAlpin Professor of Practical Theology at Union Theological Seminary. She has received many honors, including the International Council of Christians and Jews Sir Sigmund Sternberg Award and the Shevet Achim Award from the Council of Centers on Jewish-Christian Relations. Moreover, Boys' work has been recognized by many major grants and the awarding of four honorary doctorates.

Boys, following Wiesel's admonition against stereotyping, advocates both "spiritual regret" and "holy envy." The first of these terms is an acknowledgment that a variety of legitimate religious ideals exist and no one person or tradition can encompass all of them. This is one of the guiding principles behind her ground-breaking volume *Has God Only One Blessing?* "Holy envy" is a term suggested by the Swedish theologian and Bishop of Stockholm Krister Stendahl. Boys defines the term in a manner that goes a long way toward defining authentic interfaith dialogue. She writes: "The experience of something so profound in the beliefs, rituals, polity, or practices of another tradition that one wishes her or his own community of faith also had (or practiced) it and yet refrains out of respect for the other."[59]

ROBERT MCAFEE BROWN

Brown, a Presbyterian minister and theologian who taught at several universities including Stanford, Union Theological Seminary, and Pacific School of Religion, served on the United States Holocaust Memorial Council, which Wiesel initially chaired. Brown also accompanied the Wiesels to Oslo when Elie received the Nobel Peace Prize. Brown's 1989 book *Elie Wiesel: Messenger to All Humanity* is a Protestant scholar's reading of Wiesel. Brown's work acknowledges Wiesel's impact on Christianity. In the volume's Epilogue Brown writes to his friend:

> You have said that to be a Jew means to testify; such must also be the obligation of a Christian. And you have taught us all—Jews, Christians, and all humanity—that before testifying ourselves, we must listen to the testimony of others. I have tried to listen to your testimony. And now I feel obligated . . . to testify.[60]

Brown correctly interpreted Wiesel as both storyteller and messenger. The roles are irretrievably linked. Their implications for Christianity, the lessons, so to speak, of the Holocaust, are manifold. Among the most prominent for Americans are a commitment to justice, the staying power of faith, and a rejection of hate. Among Brown's legion of students was Mary Boys, the distinguished Catholic scholar and Union Seminary professor. As an astute interpreter of Wiesel's teachings, Brown's voice rose to prominence in Protestant theological circles. This does not mean the message was always acted on, or at some points verged on hagiography, although I do not subscribe to the hagiography accusation. However, it does mean that Wiesel's challenging message was definitely heard.

HARRY JAMES CARGAS

Cargas, who, as noted, described himself as a post-Auschwitz Catholic, was a longtime faculty member at Webster University in St. Louis. He called upon Rome to enact a series of 16 reforms which he hoped would provide the groundwork for authentic dialogue between the church and the Jewish people. Among his suggestions was the excommunication of Hitler, which did not happen. Cargas, who died in 1998, initially became acquainted with Wiesel when reading an excerpt from *Night* that was published in *Jubilee*, a now defunct Catholic magazine. Cargas confided that he wept the first time he read Wiesel's work. He and Wiesel collaborated on several books including *Harry James Cargas in Conversation With Elie Wiesel* and *Conversations With Elie Wiesel*. Consequently, he became an ardent pupil of Wiesel's thought. The dedication page of the second book reads: "The preparation for this book has been one of the holiest experiences of my life. Elie Wiesel, the man, and Elie Wiesel the writer, has given me this extended sacred moment."[61]

The discussions between Cargas, the influential Catholic thinker, and Wiesel, Holocaust survivor and Nobel Peace laureate, reveal the contours of authentic post-Shoah dialogue: intensity, honesty, and openness. The first discussion took place in 1976 at Webster University; the second occurred 16 years later at the same location. Discussions continued in interview settings at conferences held at various universities. Based on his interchanges with Wiesel, Cargas relentlessly pursued the goal of compelling the church to confront its own role in preparing the way for the Holocaust. He also prodded Catholic leaders to speak up and to speak out concerning the churches' silence during the Holocaust. Cargas, following Wiesel's admonition that the murderers were Christian, was ashamed and angry that nearly every Jew murdered in the Shoah was killed by someone who was baptized as a Christian. He continually struggled to get the church to acknowledge this fact, including the controversial role played by Pope Pius XII—the church leader before, during, and after the Shoah—in order to begin the long process of atonement necessary for authentic dialogue to begin.

FRANKLIN H. LITTELL

Franklin H. Littell was frequently referred to as the grandfather of Holocaust Studies in America. The late Protestant scholar (died 2009) believed—with Wiesel—that the Shoah presented Christianity with a massive credibility crisis, terming the Holocaust an "Alpine Event." He had spent a decade in post-war Germany as Chief Protestant Religious Advisor to the High Command specializing in the de-Nazification process. In 1970, Littell, along with the late African American scholar and clergyman Hubert Locke, organized the first Holocaust conference in America, "The Holocaust and the Church Struggle," which has met annually since then. It regularly brings together Holocaust survivors and distinguished scholars to address various concerns emerging from the Shoah. Wiesel was an honorary board member of this conference.

In 1974 attendees at the conference witnessed an exchange between Wiesel and the prominent Jewish theologian Richard Rubenstein. Rubenstein, writing in his 1966 book *After Auschwitz*, proclaimed that "God is dead." By this he meant the disappearance of all moral restraint after Auschwitz. No contemporary King David, i.e., political leader, has to worry about being admonished by a Nathan the prophet. See II Samuel 12:1–12, which refers to prophets speaking truth to power in reference to the sometimes arbitrary and immoral power wielded by the king. Moreover, we live, attests Rubenstein, in a cold, silent, indifferent universe. The connection between heaven and earth has been irreparably destroyed. Wiesel replied by making two telling points: God's death was announced not by a survivor, but by a non-witness and, he continued, if you want to really confront the theological legacy of Auschwitz, try living not without, but *with* God. Rubenstein, an ordained rabbi, then gave Wiesel a blessing.

Wiesel's indictment of Christianity's institutional failure during the Holocaust found ready expression among many of the papers delivered at Littell and Locke's annual conference. Wiesel himself delivered several keynote talks at these conferences. Littell, far from Wiesel's soft voice, thundered his indictment of the church's moral complicity in the persecution of the Jews. He accused the cooperating Protestant pastors of apostasy. His book *The Crucifixion of the Jews*, first written in 1975 and since republished, compelled thoughtful Christians to examine what went wrong with their tradition. The volume also led Jews to seek more meaningful interaction with their Christian colleagues.

FA. JOHN PAWLIKOWSKI

Professor Pawlikowski, a Servite priest, is a member of the Roman Catholic Servite Order, who has long been active in Christian-Jewish dialogue. Basing himself on an unblinking look at the deeply troubled history of Christian anti-Judaism, Pawlikowski nonetheless makes a distinction between Christian theological contempt for Judaism and Nazism's racial hatred of Jews and Judaism. The Detroit-born priest's university student years coincided with Vatican II and the promulgation of N.A. A prodigious author and tireless lecturer—both in America and abroad—he has worked extensively on deepening and expanding Vatican II's vision of interreligious dialogue. Pawlikowski was also a friend of, and co-worker with, Elie Wiesel.

President Jimmy Carter appointed Pawlikowski a founding member of the United States Holocaust Memorial Council. But first Pawlikowski had to write a letter to Elie Wiesel disavowing any plan to whitewash Polish Holocaust responsibility. This appointment was subsequently renewed by Presidents George H.W. Bush and Bill Clinton. Pawlikowski was, until his retirement, a professor of Social Ethics at Catholic Theological Union where he also directed the university's Cardinal Bernardin Center for Theology and Ministry and its Catholic-Jewish Studies program until his recent retirement. Pawlikowski received many honors and awards such as the presidency of the International Council of Christians and Jews, one of the ICCJ's honorary presidencies for his outstanding contributions to furthering positive relations between the Jewish and Christian communities, the Catholic Theological Society's 2014 John Courtney Murray Award, and an honorary doctorate from Australian Catholic University.

Pawlikowski's relationship with Wiesel began with the 1974 International Conference on the Holocaust initiated by Wiesel at the Cathedral of the St. John Divine, where Pawlikowski was one of the speakers. Following this experience, the two worked together for over a decade at the United States Holocaust Memorial Museum. Fa. Pawlikowski confides that he discovered in Wiesel the same characteristics described by Professor Carolyn Ross Johnston, who co-taught with Wiesel at Eckhardt College: teaching through storytelling, asking questions and listening to responses, recognizing that "indifference" is the opposite of love, the continuing need for moral witness, and continuing resilience.

Pawlikowski endorses Wiesel's insistence on knowing the details of the church's insistence on the Teaching of Contempt for 1,900 years. Among the Holocaust's contemporary lessons, attests Pawlikowski, is the danger of violent religious language "which can 'soften' a society for genocide."[62] Moreover, continued study of the Holocaust will enable the church to engage in a "refined self-definition" that will permit it to "stand at the forefront of a defense of human dignity that escaped it during the dark night of the Holocaust." It is well to remember at this point that Pawlikowski applauds Wiesel's support of the creation of a Committee on Conscience, whose mission would be to alert the public to an awareness of contemporary genocidal situations.

Carol Rittner, RSM (Religious Sisters of Mercy)

Rittner was the inaugural director of The Elie Wiesel Foundation for Humanity. In this capacity she oversaw several of the Foundation's initiatives, including the Elie Wiesel Prize in ethics essay contest, which is open to all college and university juniors and seniors. (See Chapter 6 of this book.) Prior to that time, Wiesel invited her to be a member of an Advisory Committee to the United States Holocaust Memorial Council. Rittner attested that

> the teacher whose lesson I am still trying to learn is Pope John XXIII. It was this old man, faithful to his church yet unafraid to confront, its past, who taught me that I have 'every right to more than hope' that the future will be different, if I am not afraid to take history seriously, to engage in dialogue with my brothers and sisters in the human family, to learn from them and to change.[63]

Moreover, she admitted to being shattered by Victor Frankl's book, *Man's Search for Meaning*, and wondered how could human beings funnel Jews into gas chambers and burn their bodies in ovens? Furthermore, this engendered other queries: "Where were the churches? Where were the Christians? Why didn't they help the Jews?"[64] She also had not yet realized in the early 1960s that "Hitler and his henchmen built their deadly ideology on the twin foundations of racist antisemitism and anti-Judaism in Christian theology."[65]

In the mid-'70s Rittner dove into Wiesel's books, took McAfee Brown's course on Wiesel, and studied in Yad Vashem, Israel's Holocaust memorial museum and research center. Subsequently, she "offered one of the earliest courses on the Holocaust to be taught at a Catholic college."[66] Wiesel's impact on Rittner is clear. In addition to her concern for authenticity in Jewish-Christian dialogue, she wrote extensively on women in the Holocaust, theological issues emerging from the Shoah, and other genocides in the twentieth and twenty-first centuries.

Wiesel invited Rittner to be a member of an advisory committee to the United States Holocaust Memorial Council, which was the precursor of the United States Holocaust Memorial Museum. Rittner was instrumental in helping organize a number of conferences including "Faith in Human Kind: Rescuers of Jews During the Holocaust." Rittner writes: "I think [Elie] was somewhat curious as to why a Roman Catholic nun was so interested and committed to learning about the Holocaust and to teaching others about it."[67] Rittner was the initial director of The Elie Wiesel Foundation for Humanity, serving for three and a half years. She worked closely with Wiesel in planning four international conferences held in Paris, Boston, Oslo, and Haifa.

John K. Roth

Roth is a veteran dialogue partner of Elie Wiesel. Early on, Roth wrote in the Preface to his 1979 book *A Consuming Fire: Encounters With Elie Wiesel and the Holocaust*: "As a Christian and as an American, I am convinced that profound encounters with God, mediated by the Holocaust as seen by Elie Wiesel, lie in store for any persons like me who will look." Roth was designated National Professor of the Year by the Carnegie Foundation for the Advancement of Teaching (1988). Wiesel visited Roth's classes at Claremont McKenna College, on many occasions interacting with students and other faculty, as well as delivering public lectures. Moreover, Wiesel was one of three internationally prominent figures (the other two were Mary Robinson, former president of Ireland, and Stuart Eizenstat, involved with Holocaust reparations in the administration of President Jimmy Carter) who were named board members of Claremont's Center for the Study of the Holocaust, Genocide, and Human Rights which, in April 2015, became the Mgrublian Center for Human Rights. Roth has discerned several lessons that Wiesel teaches for Christians, including the importance of a *din Torah* (trial of God) from *within* the tradition. This is best summarized by Wiesel's aphorism: "With God or against God, but not without God."

Roth reports an experience which serves simultaneously to bond and to differentiate the Holocaust survivor and the American professor:

> In two weeks, I read all of Wiesel's books that had thus far been published in English. The collision I experienced then between my good fortune—fatherhood, a promising academic career at Claremont McKenna College and—the destruction of family and hope explored in Wiesel's Holocaust—related reflections left lasting marks upon me.[68]

Among Wiesel's other contributions to the Jewish-Christian dialogue is fresh insight into Judaism on the part of Christian dialogue partners. As Roth attests, "Wiesel calls into question Christianity's conventional wisdom about Judaism," which relied on negative stereotypes and the assertion that Judaism has been replaced by the Christian tradition, and that Christians are the sole recipients of God's love.[69] After Auschwitz, writes Roth, "Wiesel helps us Christians to see . . . that the genuine Christian must give priority to mending the world and to repairing Christian-Jewish relations in particular."[70] In addition, Wiesel, as noted, referred to authentic Christians who did try to help the Jewish people in the kingdom of night. If there had been more of these righteous people, far more Jewish lives would have been saved.

Perhaps Wiesel's central teaching lies in his capacity to protest. Roth terms him a "protestant." Moreover, notes Roth, "Jewish 'Protestantism' is far older [and] often more profound than its more recent Christian versions."[71] Wiesel as pro-*test-ant* protests against injustice both human and divine. Roth summarizes the primary themes of a Jewish protestant:

> Faithfulness must contain allegiance to God that includes disappointment with God's use of power. Affirmation of the importance of grace must be balanced with honesty that yearns for human well-being and thus strives for God/against God.[72]

Roth attests that his own "ongoing quarrel with God, Jesus, and Christianity does not repudiate them but instead reveals what the New Testament, reflecting its Jewish roots, calls a hunger and thirst for righteousness."[73]

WIESEL'S PRO-TEST-ANT-ISM

Wiesel's pro-test-ant-ism also mandates abolishing hatred of the other; anger is acceptable, hatred is not. His *protest from within* enabled Wiesel to argue for man and against God. The road to God, for Wiesel, leads through humanity. Moreover, his protest was based on speaking out from a particular Jewish perspective which, in turn, has universal implications. He wrote as a Jew which, for him, meant that

> in accordance with my tradition, I wish to convert no one, just as I do not wish anyone to convert me. A Jew's aim is not to convert another to his faith, but to help him become more fully who he is.[74]

Writing in *A Jew Today*, Wiesel was very clear about how Christians and Jews can dialogue authentically:

> And I feel closer to certain Christians—as long as they do not try to convert me to their faith—than to certain Jews. I felt closer to John XXIII and to François Mauriac than to self-hating Jews. I have more in common with an authentic and tolerant Christian than with a Jew who is neither authentic nor tolerant.[75]

Wiesel's stress on questions—which contains the word quest—allows the dialogue to continue. Questions express common human aspirations and fears. Moreover, as a storyteller Wiesel could raise and re-raise questions. Answers, however, can be fatal. They either reject or block out the Other. The Nazis had an answer they called the Final Solution, which resulted in the death of six million Jews. Jesus died with a question on his lips, "My lord, why hast thou forsaken me?" Moreover, as we have stressed, it is significant that the Hebrew word for question—*she'elah*—contains the name of God—El. As noted, by questing together humans come closer to each other and to the divine.

CRITICISM OF WIESEL'S POSITION

Not everyone in the Jewish and Christian communities applauds Wiesel's dialogical efforts. Three groups oppose interfaith dialogue: ultra-right-wing Christians and Jews, and Jews for Jesus. The Jewish and Christian extremists have no interest in dialogue, although for different reasons. Extremist Jewish groups such as the *Naturei Karta* (N.K.) in Israel, who see themselves as guardians of normative Jewish teachings, oppose any interaction with those outside of their own group. This applies to the State of Israel as well. The N.K. are opposed to the secular State of Israel because it was built by human hands and not the Messiah. In America, the Satmar Hasidim, ideologically allied with *Naturei Karta*, view themselves as the last hoop on the barrel of chaos. They have nothing to do with non-Satmar Jews, let alone the prospect of interfaith dialogue.

Christian right-wing Evangelicals are, by and large, not interested in dialogue. For the most part, their concern is with gathering all Jews into the land of Israel where they will be given a last chance to convert prior to the Second Coming of Jesus. This position is similar to the Church of Latter-Day Saints, which insists on converting dead Jews to membership. If the Jews fail to see the theological light, i.e., acknowledge the messiahship of Jesus, they will face eternal damnation.

The Jews for Jesus movement espouses a theologically confused point of view, claiming that they alone have correctly understood the Hebrew Bible. This claim is bolstered both by selectively citing the Bible and by taking quotes out of context. The Jews for Jesus movement is shunned by mainstream Jewish and Christian groups. What all three of the opposition groups share is their unwillingness or inability to permit theological self-definition to the religious Other.

CONCLUSION

Wiesel has had an enormous impact on Christian-Jewish dialogue in America. His death was mourned by people of many faith communities; rabbis, ministers, and priests eulogized him. The American context itself is important. The country as a whole endorses Jewish-Christian dialogue; annual conferences are held, Jewish and Christian leaders speak at each other's houses of worship, colleges and universities have courses related to the dialogue. Moreover, the dialogue occurs both on the scholarly and lay levels. Leaders of professional Jewish organizations such as the American Jewish Committee and the anti-Defamation League regularly interact with Vatican leadership. This activity can be broadly subsumed under the mantle of America's concern for civil and human rights. In addition, many Christian thinkers who have been influenced by Wiesel's message are teachers who have influenced countless thousands of students who, in turn, become messengers as in Wiesel's aphorism: "To listen to a witness is to become a witness."

Wiesel's interfaith teachings are based on the fact that the Holocaust shattered all pre-Shoah paradigms. People of good will need to emphasize the necessity for a new beginning. This new start requires, at a minimum, respect for the religious Other. Moreover, Wiesel has pointed to the fact that Christianity needs Judaism to cleanse itself of the disease of antisemitism in a way that refrains from punishing or blaming contemporary Christians who make sincere efforts at redefining their tradition in a way that avoids both theological triumphalism (Christianity is morally and theologically superior to Judaism) and the claim that Christianity supersedes Judaism. For Wiesel, no religion was superior. But all religious people need to interrogate the deity on behalf of humanity.

Wiesel's example creates a relationship with Christians within the context of a safe environment. Christians, by problematizing their own tradition and grappling with those portions of their sacred text that preach hatred, become pro-test-ants in the true sense of that word. Genuine dialogue eschews conversion. Wiesel attested to the fact that the Holocaust was a paradigm shattering event which compels all people of faith to rethink basic principles. His call for interfaith dialogue, as we have seen, presupposes that God is always present in authentic interfaith interchange.

This sets the bar very high. But it is a necessary standard in an uncertain world facing a multitude of complex issues. Wiesel as the *maggid* (preacher) of Sighet is a messenger to both Christians and Jews that a better mutual understanding is indeed possible and necessary. Moreover, Wiesel's example of dialogue made possible public discussion of religion without rancor. Lack of respect for this position was one of the many contemporary worrying signs of the Trump administration with its adherence to conspiracy theories, ridicule of the Other, and lack of civility, all three of which stand in the strongest possible contrast to what Wiesel advocated. The 2020 election of President Joseph R. Biden holds the promise of a brighter and far less corrosive and politically fraught atmosphere. Authentic dialogue acknowledges a necessary relationship between *particular* identity and *universal* meaning, whose implications embrace all those striving for a deeper understanding of the faith of others as well as that of their own tradition.

In the next chapter we discuss Wiesel's works on the second generation, seeking how memory of the Shoah is transmitted and altered.

NOTES

1. Elie Wiesel and Richard D. Heffner, *Conversations With Elie Wiesel*. Edited by Thomas J. Vinciguerra. New York: Schocken Books, 2003, page 61.
2. Ibid.
3. Elie Wiesel, *A Jew Today*. Translated by Marion Wiesel. New York: Vintage Books, 1979, page 13.
4. Harry James Cargas, *Conversations With Elie Wiesel*. South Bend: Justice Books, 1992, page 47. Hereafter this work will be cited as *Conversations*.
5. It is significant that the University of Notre Dame Press has published at least two other works dealing with Wiesel: Alan Rosen, *Celebrating Elie Wiesel: Stories, Essays, Reflections*. Notre Dame, IN: University of Notre Dame Press, 1998; Robert McAfee Brown, *Elie Wiesel: Messenger to All Humanity*. Notre Dame, IN: University of Notre Dame Press, 1989.
6. Jonathan Sarna, *American Judaism: A History*. New Haven: Yale University Press, 2004, page 267. Hereafter this work will be cited as *AJ*.
7. This remark has been widely attributed to President Eisenhower, although no direct source seems to exist.
8. Elie Wiesel, *All Rivers Run to the Sea*. New York: Alfred A. Knopf, 1995, page 69. Wiesel pays tribute to Maria and to Maria-type figures in the following volumes: *The Fifth Son*, *The Trial of God*, *The Sonderberg Case*, and *The Time of the Uprooted*.
9. Elie Wiesel, *Night*. Translated by Marion Wiesel. New York: Hill and Wang, 2006, page 41.
10. Ibid., page 4.

11. Cited by John K. Roth, *A Consuming Fire: Encounters With Elie Wiesel and the Holocaust.* Atlanta: John Knox Press, 1979.

12. Elie Wiesel, *And the Sea Is Never Full.* Translated by Marion Wiesel. New York: Alfred A. Knopf, 1999, page 169.

13. Wiesel's reflection on whether or not the covenant was broken during the Holocaust leaves a great deal of room for theological ambiguity. He told Harry James Cargas, "I believe during the Holocaust the covenant was broken. Maybe it will be renewed; perhaps later, maybe it was renewed even then, on a different level. So many Jews kept their faith or even strengthened it. But it was broken, because of the clouds and because of the fire." However, elsewhere he observes that even in Auschwitz he continued to believe in God—the source of the covenant. *Conversations,* pages 56–57.

14. Elie Wiesel, *Legends of Our Time.* New York: Schocken Books, 1982, page 190.

15. *AJ,* page 266.

16. Ibid., 267.

17. Ellen Fine, *Legacy of Night.* Albany: SUNY Press, 1982, page 58.

18. Deborah E. Lipstadt, *Holocaust: An American Understanding.* New Brunswick: Rutgers University Press, 2016, page 41.

19. Elie Wiesel, "Elie Wiesel and Interfaith Dialogue," in *Elie Wiesel: Teacher, Mentor, and Friend.* Edited by Alan L. Berger. Eugene, OR: Cascade Books, 2018, page 77.

20. Ibid.

21. Irving Abrahamson (editor), *Against Silence: The Voice and Vision of Elie Wiesel.* New York: Holocaust Library, 1985, volume I, page 131.

22. Ibid.

23. *Conversations,* page 48.

24. Alan L. Berger, "Interview of Elie Wiesel," *Literature and Belief,* 2014, 26, no. 1, page 19.

25. Ibid., page 16.

26. Ibid., page 14.

27. Ibid., page 13.

28. Ibid., page 14.

29. Elie Wiesel. *The Sonderberg Case.* Knopf Doubleday Publishing Group 2010. page 165

30. Wiesel, "Elie Wiesel and Interfaith Dialogue," page 78.

31. *Conversations,* page 165.

32. Frederick Downing, *Elie Wiesel: A Religious Biography.* Macon, GA: Mercer University Press, 2008, page 172.

33. Ibid., page 177.

34. Elie Wiesel, *The Gates of the Forest.* Translated by Frances Frenaye. New York: Schocken Books, page 199.

35. Ibid., page 198.

36. McAfee Brown, *Elie Wiesel: Messenger to All Humanity,* page 92.

37. *Conversations,* page 47.

38. Victoria Aarons, "'The Past Became the Present,' Reenactment of Trauma in Elie Wiesel's *The Gates of the Forest,*" *Literature and Belief,* 2006, 26, no. 1, page 55.

39. Wiesel, Elie *The Gates of the Forest,* Knopf Doubleday Publishing Group page 60.

40. Elie Wiesel *The Gates of the Forest.* Knopf Doubleday Publishing Group. Page 133. 1995.

41. Elie Wiesel. *The Time of the Uprooted.* Translated by David Hapgood. Knopf Doubleday Publishing Group. 2007. page. 60

42. Ibid.

43. Wiesel, *All Rivers,* page 69.

44. Carole J. Lambert, *The Judges.* New York: Alfred A. Knopf, 1999, page 96.

45. *Conversations,* page 33.

46. Downing, *Elie Wiesel,* page 101.

47. "First encounter with François Mauriac." Elie Wiesel collection, Gottlieb Archives, Mugar Library. Boston University, B. 260, F.23. no date. The French original reads, "En cet instant de verité, je choisis de personnifier le justicier juif, tandis que lui, l'ecrivain chretien au faite de la glorie et comble de honneurs et de certitudes, incarnait pour moi le monde chretien tout entire, depuis son origine et Jusqu's nos jours, son histoire et sa rute, ses rois et ses pretres qui basent leur foi sur la mort d'un juif, sur la mort des juifs. J'allai m'ecrie ne pleurez pas, il est trop tard, toutes les larmes de tous les chrestiens ne pourront effacer le sang verse."

48. *Conversations*, page 43.

49. Irving Abrahamson (editor), *Against Silence: The Voice and Wisdom of Elie Wiesel*. New York: Holocaust Library, 1985, volume III, page 110.

50. Wiesel, *All Rivers*, page 268.

51. Ibid., 269.

52. Wiesel, *And the Sea Is Never Full*, page 167.

53. Ibid., page 169.

54. Elie Wiesel and John Cardinal O'Connor, *A Journey of Faith*. Edited by Gabe Pressman. New York: Primus, 1990, page 39.

55. Ibid.

56. Roberto Suro, "John Paul Holds Waldheim Meeting," *New York Times*, June 26, 1987, page 2.

57. Alan L. Berger, "Interview With Elie Wiesel," in *The Continuing Agony: From the Carmelite Convent to the Crosses at Auschwitz*. Edited by Alan L. Berger, Harry J. Cargas, and Susan E. Nowak. Academic Studies in the History of Judaism. Binghamton, NY: Binghamton University Press, 2002, page 280.

58. Ibid., 281.

59. Janet Clair, "Common Ground and Holy Ground: Prayers of the Holocaust," in *Remembering for the Future*. (eds(=) John K. Roth, Elisabeth Maxwel, Margot Levy, Wendy Whitworth. London: Palgrave Macmillan, 2001, volume I, page 405.

60. McAfee Brown, *Elie Wiesel: Messenger to All Humanity*, Epilogue, no page number.

61. *Conversations*, dedication page, no page number.

62. Fa. John Pawlikowski, "Creating an Ethical Context for Globalization: Catholic Perspectives in an Interreligious Context," *Journal of Ecumenical Studies*, 2007, 42, no. 3, pages 363–372.

63. Carol Rittner. "From Ignorance to Insight in *From the Unthinkable to the Unavoidable: American Christians and Jewish Scholars encounter the Holocaust* edited by Carol Rittner and John K. Roth. Westport, CT. Greenwood Press, 1997, page 135.

64. Ibid., 69.

65. Ibid.

66. Ibid., page 68.

67. Carol Rittner, "Afterword," in *Elie Wiesel: Teacher, Mentor, and Friend*. Edited by Alan L. Berger. Eugene, OR: Cascade Books, 2018, page 91.

68. Berger, "Interview With Elie Wiesel," page 39.

69. John Roth, "Wiesel's Contribution to a Christian Understanding of Judaism," in *Elie Wiesel: Jewish, Literary, and Moral Perspectives*. Edited by Steven T. Katz and Alan Rosen. Bloomington: Indiana University Press, 2013, page 265.

70. Ibid., page 267.

71. Ibid., page 269.

72. Ibid.

73. John K. Roth, *Sources of Holocaust Insight: Learning and Teaching About the Genocide*. Eugene, OR: Cascade Books, 2020, page 44.

74. Wiesel, *And the Sea Is Never Full*, page 169.

75. Wiesel, *A Jew Today*, page 13.

CHAPTER 3

THE SECOND GENERATION

MEMORY AND JEWISH IDENTITY

Memory plays a vital role in transmitting and retaining Jewish identity. It is the keystone of this identity, linking the generations and fortifying membership in the community. Professor Yosef Hayim Yerushalmi reminds readers that the verb *zakhor* (to remember), or its linguistic variants, appears "one hundred and sixty-nine times in the Hebrew Bible."[1] Furthermore, both covenantal partners—Israel and God—are required to remember. Judaism has in fact been described as a "technology of memory." Wiesel stresses the post-Shoah role played by memory, comparing it to the theological glue holding Jewish identity together. He writes, "If we stop remembering, we stop being."[2] More to the point, claims of memory lead inexorably to actions in the world: *zachor v'shamor b'dibar echad*, remembering and observing are the same thing, argued the rabbis. Consequently, Wiesel's call for memory means a call for action in the world; protests against injustice, standing with the victims, speaking out in support of those who have no voice, and standing up against hate. See Chapter 5 for a fuller discussion of this matter.

But it is significant to note that Jewish memory itself undergoes a profound change. In modernity, for the first time, Yerushalmi notes, many contemporary Jews "are in search of a past," but not the one "offered by the historian."[3] History and memory are in a tense and not always creative relationship. One can be objective about history. This is not the case for memory. For example, despite historical and archaeological evidence that the story of the Exodus in the Bible never happened the way it is presented, Jews still observe the Passover Seder, in which they are commanded to personally feel as if they themselves are liberated from bondage. Turning specifically to the Shoah, he writes, "the Holocaust [has] engendered more historical research than any single event in Jewish history, but . . . its image is being shaped, not at the historian's anvil, but in the novelist's crucible."[4] Jews, he contends, "are not prepared to confront history directly, but seem to await a new metahistorical myth, for which the novel provides at least a temporary modern surrogate."[5] Memory is more existentially powerful than history. Wiesel is both storyteller (*maggid* in Hebrew) of Hasidism and witness to the Shoah; like Job's messengers, he can say, "I alone have escaped to tell you" (Job 1:15, 17, 19). The Nobel Peace laureate is well suited to be the post-modern chronicler of the Holocaust and what he views as its contemporary lessons for American culture.

On the one hand, memory transmission is of course still rooted in the Hebrew bible, the book that Isaac Bashevis Singer describes as having hypnotized the Jewish people forever, and its many commandments to remember. Prophesizing in the wake of a devastating locust attack, the prophet Joel admonished his listeners:

> Hear this, you aged men,
> Give ear, all inhabitants of the
> Land!
> Has such a thing happened in your
> Days,
> Or in the days of your fathers?
> Tell your children of it,
> And let your children tell their
> Children,
> And their children another
> generation.

(Joel 1:2–3)

The prophet specifies four generations who will interrogate normative teachings of the tradition and ask questions: Has God abandoned us? Is the covenant still valid? Have we sinned? How can we repair our relationship with God?

On the other hand, and unlike the prophet Joel, National Socialism wanted no Jew left alive to tell of the disaster that engulfed their generation and the Nazi crimes that engendered so much human suffering. Wiesel attested that the "[Shoah] was essentially a war against memory."[6] The Nazis said they "wanted a world without Jews, a world without Jewish memory."[7] It is true that with certain exceptions—Wiesel among them—a 20-year "curtain of silence"—at least on the part of novelists—descended on discussion of the Shoah following the conclusion of the war.

It is, however, necessary to point out that in 1945 President Truman issued an executive order to allow displaced persons into the U.S. and in 1948 Congress finally changed immigration laws to allow DP's (Displaced Persons) into America. In 1953 the Refugee Relief Act brought many survivors to America. The diary of Anne Frank was published in Dutch in 1947 and in English in 1952. A play on Broadway and a movie in 1959 won three Oscars. However, Anne's diary in the Broadway version was presented as a "feel good" play that omitted the tragedy of her situation. By this time, the Anne Frank House was a museum in Amsterdam. Yad Vashem opened in 1953, which was a major commitment to a museum for a young country. This was also the case with Leon Uris's popular novel *Exodus* (1958) and its cinematic presentation two years later that received an Oscar. Things began to change with a fuller understanding of the Holocaust among American Jewry when the Eichmann kidnapping and subsequent trial in Israel in 1960–1962 drove home the agony and awfulness of the Holocaust. The sheer horror of the Shoah stood in sharp contrast to America's impatience with history and its desire for a quick fix. In any case, the Holocaust caused a caesura between what came before and what emerged in the aftermath.

Wiesel faced a conundrum; the Shoah's victims must be spoken about, but to speak about them is to betray them. Wiesel's dialogue between speech and silence was discussed in Chapter 2. In addition, Wiesel writes in *One Generation After*: "Tell them [Holocaust survivors] that silence, more than language, remains the substance and the seal of what was once their universe, and that, like language, demands to be recognized and transmitted."[8] Wiesel's work is suffused with the conflict between speech and silence. He contended that like the Torah, which is written in black ink on white parchment, both the black and the white need to be communicated. In one example from *Night* following the scene in which a son kills his father for a crust of bread and is, in turn, murdered by others, Wiesel writes, "I was sixteen years old." This is a type of silence pregnant with meaning. Moreover, there was no widely accepted communal myth that was applicable to the destruction of six million Jews. Classical explanations failed in the face of the Holocaust. Neither the biblical *mi'penei hateinu* (we are exiled from the land because of our sins) nor the rabbinic *yessurin shel ahavah* (reproof of love) seemed applicable in the wake of this hideous loss. The Talmudic assertion that the Messiah would come in a generation that was either wholly pure or totally evil also fell into the historical scrap heap. Jews had to begin anew.

In the face of this challenge children of survivors, the second generation, emerged as the leaven in the lump. It was they who were witnesses of the witnesses' continued survival and the psycho-social toll it exacted.

This generation emerged as the keepers of Judaism's torch of remembrance. There were religious people and secularists among their number, those who became religious and those who abandoned formal ritual observance. But all were united by their membership in the second generation. "The second generation," attested Wiesel, "is the most meaningful aspect of our work. Their role in a way is even more difficult than ours. They are responsible for a world they didn't create. They who did not go through the experience must transmit it."[9]

Wiesel wrote four specifically second-generation novels: *The Oath* (1973, set somewhere in Eastern Europe),[10] *The Testament* (1981, set in both Czarist and communist Russia),[11] *The Fifth Son* (1985, set in Brooklyn and Germany),[12] and *The Forgotten* (1992, set in America and Romania).[13] In literary terms, each of these works assume Jewish cultural and religious norms as the background against which the main character's actions and behavior are judged. This stands in radical opposition to novels by mainstream Jewish-American writers of the '50s and '60s. For example, see Herman Wouk's *Marjorie Morningstar* and the assimilation characters in Philip Roth's "Eli, the Fanatic," and Bernard Malamud's short story "The Lady of the Lake." Furthermore, Wiesel paints a fuller portrait of the personality of his second-generation protagonists with each succeeding novel.

The Oath deals with the survivors' struggle between speech and silence and the obligation imposed on the hearer of the tale. *The Testament* treats the self-exile of the witness, his ultimate disillusionment with the false messianism of communism, and the obligation of his mute son to bear witness. *The Fifth Son* examines the destructive motive of vengeance and its transformation into a need for moral witness bearing on the part of the second generation. *The Forgotten* has a two-fold message: a survivor afflicted with Alzheimer's disease must transmit his memories to his son before it's too late, and the novel is also a meditation on the efficacy of God's memory as well as the futility of vengeance. In the nearly two decades between the appearance of Wiesel's first and last second-generation novels, the second generation had become an established social and literary movement in America. The second-generation authors, filmmakers, and poets shared incisive insights into their psycho-social and theological Shoah legacy. On the one hand, their survivor parents had transmitted not only what they endured in the camps, but also the many questions, existential, psychological, and theological, which emerged from that conflagration. On the other hand, there were survivors who spoke rarely if at all about their Holocaust experiences. The social psychologist Yael Danielli observes that whether survivors spoke or not was largely dependent on the type of experience they had during the war. Offspring of partisan families heard stories that were heroic in nature. Death camp families told stories of a very different type. Much also depended on the personality of the survivor.

Moreover, the emergence of the second generation in America occurred against the background of the country's embrace of other ethnic or identity groups, e.g., the feminist movement, Afro-American identity (which evolved into the Black Lives Matter movement), gays and lesbians (precursors of the LGBTQ movement), and Vietnam veterans. Moreover, trauma studies began to emerge as an important scholarly field of research. I shall return briefly to the issue of American identity politics and the second generation in the discussion later in the chapter.

Reflecting on the biblical book of Job, in "Some Words for Children of Survivors: A Message to the Second Generation" in *The Holocaust 40 Years After*, Elie Wiesel raised important questions for the second generation. He attested that "the real tragedy of Job begins *after* the tragedy. At the end of Job's tale, God compensates the biblical figure. Once again, he had ten children, seven sons and three daughters. And he became a happy man. Wiesel unequivocally repudiated the story, writing, "I don't believe it."[14] What, for example, is a replacement child"? No child can be replaced. Instead, Wiesel advocated for a sequel beginning where the current tale ends. Questions abound: What happened to Job's *second* children? How could they live in a house filled with tragedy? How could Job and his wife live with their memories? More emphasis should be placed on Mrs. Job. Why is the story so short? Why the unbelievable happy ending? The real tragedy which follows the other tragedy is the tragedy of Job's children, the children of the survivors.[15] Moreover, in literary terms, the second generation employs the cultural and religious norms of Judaism as their touchstone of reality, rather than those of American culture.

Specifically concerning Job's second set of children, Wiesel had an abundance of questions.

> What did they think of the problems their parents had endured? And of their innocent brothers and sisters who had been sacrificed because, on high, there had been some doubt about Job's piety? Did they try to find out who their elder siblings had been? It was with them that Job and his wife would have lived happily if Satan and God had not made their wager.[16]

This chapter discusses Wiesel's four second-generation novels: *The Oath*, *The Testament*, *The Fifth Son*, and *The Forgotten*. Professor Daniel Stern contends that Wiesel's "second-generation" novels are *watersheds* (my emphasis) marking a unique historical moment which signaled Wiesel's "movement . . . from despair toward hope."[17] Furthermore, Stern links Wiesel's work for the freedom of Soviet Jewry (*The Jews of Silence*) and his second-generation novels. He writes: "The slaughtered millions of the Holocaust had endured their fates and were gone, but the fate of the Jews of the Soviet Union and the children of the survivors were both still in question."[18] Wiesel's second-generation novels move from a focus on remembrance of the dead to bearing witness on behalf of the living. Each of Wiesel's second-generation novels is discussed in light of his two-fold attestation that he who listens to a witness becomes a witness, and the ethical obligation that this entails. In addition, I comment on the changing paradigm of Holocaust representation in selected artistic responses of the second and third generations. The chapter concludes with an observation about the pernicious effects of Holocaust denial.

THE OATH

In this novel Wiesel tells the tale of an old man's despairing attempt to convince an anonymous youth to refrain from committing suicide. Azriel ("whom God helps"), the old man, is the sole survivor of a pogrom which destroyed his village of Kolvillag (Hebrew term signifying every village a prototype of countless Jewish European shtetls). The young man is also a survivor, the son of Holocaust victims, but he has no defining story to tell. He is a "second" only child. His parents live in the past. When they look at him they see their first-born son who was murdered in the Shoah. He reminds the reader of Wiesel's observation about the second generation: they who did not go through the experience must transmit it.

Azriel's encounter with the nameless young man signals a turning point in the novel. Going deeper psychologically, Wiesel writes of the young man, "He arouses our pity because he doesn't even have the consolation of being a witness. He represents all my students and all the young people who are so perplexed."[19] The young man, unable to communicate with his mother who continually rebukes herself for not going with her five-year-old son to the gas chamber after his "selection," wonders, "Where do I fit in? I suffered with her and for her, but I could not understand. Where do I fit in, where?"[20] The Shoah is too overwhelming for the youth. Azriel's encounter with him signifies a three-fold change; it is the beginning of his re-thinking of his oath of silence, about the fate of Kolvillag noted earlier in this chapter, it is a decision to testify in order to save a life, and it charges the young man with the sacred obligation to bear witness.

Shmuel, Azriel's father was a scribe, who described the life of Kolvillag in a Pinkas (communal archive). Prior to perishing along with the other inhabitants of the village, he transmitted the book to his son Azriel, sole survivor of the massacre, and the novel's narrator. Azriel has sworn an oath of silence to his father concerning Kolvillag's destruction. Should he violate his oath is the novel's animating question. If so, he will be placed under *Herem* (excommunication) by the souls of the dead villagers.

He has spent his life as a *Na-venadnik*, "in perpetual exile a stranger among strangers, wandering throughout Europe honoring this pledge."[21] He has seen much, including the rejection of Jewish identity in favor of the false messiah of communism. In the course of his exile, he meets Abrasha, "another kind of *Na-venadnik*." Abrasha was a Komintern agent whose mission was to organize and activate Jewish students, arm them, and organize them into a revolutionary movement. He was doing very well in his vocation. Abrasha enlists the aid of the younger and unsuspecting Azriel. The older youth was working tirelessly in order to achieve his goal, including enlisting the aid of the naïve Azriel. Suddenly, he is summoned to Moscow without explanation. He is executed in the Russian capital by those whose ideals he eagerly embraced. Jews who lust after false gods and prophets do not fare well in Wiesel's novels.

Moshe, the mad seer, had courageously volunteered to plead guilty to the murder of a Christian—which he did not commit—in order to save Kolvillag from destruction. Too late, he discovers that his sacrifice would be in vain. The Jews would still be blamed and their village destroyed. This fact leads Moshe to a radical position concerning witness bearing. He demands an oath of silence from the Jewish villagers who would thereby break the chain of transmission of Jewish memory. Essentially, Moshe argues for a reversal of the age-old pattern of Jewish response to tragedy:

> The more they hate us, the more we shout our love of man: the more they mock us, the more we shout our attachment to history. The enemy can do with us as he pleases, but never will he silence us—that has been our motto.[22]

> Put an end to it once and for all. We have been mankind's memory and heart too long. Too long have we been other nations' laughingstock. Our stories have either amused or annoyed them. Now we shall adopt a new way: silence.[23]

> "Memory insisted [Shmuel,] everything is in memory." "Silence," Moshe insisted, "everything is in silence."[24]

Azriel decides to violate his oath of silence in order to save the young man's life. He tells the tale of Kolvillag. Echoing Genesis 32:26 where Jacob is wrestling with the angel ("Let me go for the day is breaking"), Azriel speaks to the young man: "Day is breaking, you must leave." He expresses no regret at having violated his oath. But the young man has assumed a duty. Having received the story, he no longer has the right to die. Having heard the witness he, himself, is morally and ethically obligated to become a witness. The two never see each other again.

Azriel returned to die of natural causes in the young man's stead in Kolvillag. The young man assumes his mission as a second-generation witness.

Professor Michael Berenbaum correctly notes that *The Oath* reveals two major shifts in Wiesel's position. First is a re-examination of the role of witness, questioning the relative value of silence and words,[25] narrowing his expectations of the witnesses' impact from the cosmic to the personal dimension. Second, Wiesel has moved from a "protest against death to an outright appeal to life."[26] Earlier, Wiesel had wondered about the efficacy of the witness. He wrote, "Nothing has been learned; Auschwitz has not even served as a warning. For more detailed information, consult your daily newspaper."[27] Wiesel's literary work pits the theme of the unheard (ignored) witness against the absolute command to bear witness.

THE TESTAMENT

This novel is set in Russia, although Paltiel Kossover, the peripatetic protagonist, also visits Berlin, Paris, and Spain during that country's Civil War, and finally returns to Russia during World War II and after. Kossover, like *The Oath*'s Abrasha, abandons Judaism in favor of communism's allure, becoming an agent of the International Communist Party. Wiesel stresses the point that communism and antisemitism have the same name; you can live only by abandoning your Judaism. Communism is essentially a false messianism. The most forsaken of Jews are those who *self-exile* from Judaism, which is tantamount to abandoning your core identity. In the end, these exiles, when they finally re-embrace their Jewish identity, are first imprisoned by the communist regime, then executed.

Wiesel had a highly personal interest in the phenomenon of "religious Jews opting for communism."[28] How, he wondered, "could a Jew imbued with Moses and Isaiah adopt the theories or the faith of Marx and Stalin?" This remains an unanswered question. He confided: "Even my mother, pious as she was, felt the attraction of the Communist ideal."[29] Following the war, he discovered that the "laughing mustached man who [visited] the [Wiesels'] store when things were slow . . . was an underground Communist activist." Wiesel wondered if this was the reason that "at one point she abandoned the broadcasts of Radio London for those of Radio Moscow."[30]

Based on the lives of the murdered poet Peretz Markish and the novelist Der Nister, *The Testament* is among the most historically rich of Wiesel's novels; it is essentially a warning against chasing after false gods and a summons to re-embrace one's Jewish identity.[31] Paltiel ("God is my refuge" and "I am a refugee from God"; the double meaning of this name refers to the tension between faith and doubt, which is a potential in every person) began as a religious Jew. He leaves his mute son, Grisha, a nickname for Gershon (the Gershonites were identified with the Tabernacle and, later, the Jerusalem Temple), a testament he wrote while imprisoned and awaiting execution on Stalin's orders. The document, which is essentially a testament of repentance, rejects his earlier embrace of communism, which he now rightfully terms "Godless messianism." Moreover, the document is a mature embrace of *Ahavat Yisrael*—love of the Jewish people. Wiesel observes of the testament, "written in prison, this document frees others from prison."[32] Implicit in Wiesel's prison imagery is the illusion of any and all redemptive systems that deny the sacrality of human life, choosing instead to seek refuge in abstractions like "humanity" rather than in easing the suffering of flesh and blood human beings. Paltiel's journeys had revealed the extent to which the Jewish people had been abandoned and betrayed, eventually being murdered in the Shoah.

Grisha has not seen his father since he was two years old. Five years later, he intentionally had bitten off his tongue so as not to betray Paltiel. Viktor Zupenof, the jailor who sympathizes with Paltiel, brings the prisoner paper and pen so that he can complete his manuscript. He also smuggles the manuscript out of the prison and serves as a father figure to the young Grisha, who exclaims, "My father is a book and books do not die (page 39)." Zupenof tells the youth, "You will speak on behalf of your dead father."[33] Grisha makes *aliyah* to Israel on the eve of the Yom Kippur war, bringing along Paltiel's testament. Yom Kippur signifies the end of the year-long cycle of reading the Torah and the anticipation of beginning anew. This symbolically instantiates Paltiel's testimony in Judaism's annual ritual cycle, ensuring that his tale will, with Grisha's help, become part of the warp and woof of Jewish history.

Symbolically, Wiesel's *Testament* establishes the crucial distinction between survivors and their offspring. The survivor is the one who has experienced the horror which authorizes him/her to bear witness. Grisha is mute. The second generation's muteness stands for the distinction between memory and experience. Literally unable to speak, his son will memorize then transmit Paltiel's memory in Israel. The second generation at this juncture assumes increasing responsibility for transmitting Holocaust memories, thereby strengthening Jewish identity and negating a false universalism which seeks to obliterate this identity.

THE FIFTH SON

The Fifth Son, published in 1985 in America, is a novel set against the cultural turbulence of the previous two decades in various countries: America, Czechoslovakia, and France. Focusing on America, one saw nightly news programs showing left-wing students rebelling against traditional values, searching instead for means of overthrowing the establishment in order to achieve social justice; cities burning; and the Democratic National Convention in Chicago as the scene of both a police riot and the trial of the Chicago Seven, led by Abbie Hoffman and Jerry Rubin.

Academic discussions were deemed irrelevant; "everything that was linked to the past, [university students] rejected scornfully."[34] Furthermore, the novel explores the dynamics between physical and moral vengeance within the psychologically fraught relationship between a survivor, Reuven ("see a son"—Hebrew) Tamiroff, and Ariel, his second-born "only" son.

Wiesel dedicated *The Fifth Son* to his own son, Elisha, and to all other children of survivors. This was his first second-generation novel in which a survivor seeks to portray both the inner psychic life of the second generation and the fraught father-son relationship. Wiesel emphasized the significance of his relationship with the second generation, many of whom were his students. "[When] they come to me and they say," We cannot speak to our parents because our parents don't talk or talk poorly or they are too shy. Because of you, we understand our parents." Then, Wiesel writes, "I feel reconciled to my work."[35]

The Tamiroff family suffers greatly from their Holocaust experience: Ariel's mother is institutionalized, his father is withdrawn and silent, and Ariel—like the nameless youth in *The Oath*—wonders where he fits into the Holocaust. Moreover, the novel links Holocaust memory to the Passover Seder. The *Haggadah* (text read at a Seder) speaks of four sons: the wise, the evil, the simple, and the one who doesn't know how to ask a question. In this book, the fifth son is the absent one—murdered in the Shoah. The *Haggadah*—derived from the root meaning *l'haggid* (to tell)—is the central ritual text of Passover. It commands Jews to tell and personally experience the national memory of salvation from Egyptian bondage. In just such a manner, survivor memory must "fuel the imagination" of the second generation. It is Reuven's duty to teach the American-born Ariel about the Shoah.

Wiesel's linking of the Passover Seder and its *Haggadah* with the Shoah highlights the difference between the foundational salvific event in Jewish history—the Exodus from Egypt and the redemption from slavery—and those (the Nazis) who acted to extinguish that history. The four sons to whom one is obligated to relate the tale of the Exodus symbolize attitudes toward Jewish history. The wise son models interest and wisdom in his precise questions concerning the Exodus. The wicked son fails to see any relationship between himself and the Passover rituals. He excludes the covenant event, and therefore the central story of classical Jewish identity, by asking what this service means to you—but not to him. The simple son, although sincere, is ignorant. The fourth son lacks the maturity to inquire.

Typically for survivors, their friends are fellow survivors. In Reuven's case, Bontchek and a mystic named Simha the Dark serve as guides to Ariel as he seeks to gain more knowledge about the Shoah and understanding of his father, who is portrayed as melancholy and uncommunicative. Like *The Testament*'s Paltiel Kossover, Reuven had for a time abandoned Judaism. After the Shoah, he spends much time writing letters to his murdered first-born son.

Moreover, the name Ariel is itself ambiguous. It can mean "lion or mountain of God." It can also be understood as denoting the destruction of Jerusalem. The American-born Ariel undertakes a pilgrimage to Reshastadt ("evil city") in Germany to confront Richard Lander, a Nazi commandant, responsible for the death of his brother, also named Ariel (the missing child of his parents), in the Shoah, and whom Reuven mistakenly believes he had assassinated after the Holocaust. The novel reveals Wiesel's changing attitude toward revenge. Furthermore, *The Fifth Son* distinguishes between first- and second-generation Germans. The latter are not guilty, although they are responsible for perpetuating Holocaust memory. They are obliged to "never forget."

Seeking to articulate the mission of the second generation, Wiesel casts the American-born Ariel as a professor of Holocaust Studies at a small Eastern college. The second generation thus assumes a pedagogical role in teaching generations of college students about the Shoah.

But Ariel learns that studying about the Shoah is a never-ending demand. He hears stories from Bontcheck, including the fate of the Jews in the ghetto of Davarowsk. In addition, he reads incessantly about the destruction of European Jewry and, following his paternal example, begins composing letters to his dead brother. Eventually, he travels to Reshastadt in Germany to confront the Nazi "Angel of Death," liquidator of the fictional Davarowsk ghetto. Returning to America, Ariel resumes his teaching, studying, and bearing witness to the Shoah.

Wiesel wisely distinguishes the second generation from the survivors in terms of enacting the mitzvah (commandment to pursue justice). Reuven, the survivor, had sought to assassinate his Nazi tormentor. But Ariel is the son of a survivor. He seeks out a rabbi to bless his proposed assassination mission. The rabbi contends that God alone is the true judge in this matter. This highlights the historical and experiential difference between the two generations. Ariel muses:

> I suffer from an Event I have not even experienced. A feeling of void: from a past that has made History tremble I have retained only words. War for me, is my mother's closed face. War, for me, is my father's weariness.[36]

When he finally does confront the Nazi, now a prosperous German businessman, it is not to assassinate him, but to expose his murderous past. He tells the murderer: "Wherever you are you shall feel like an intruder, pursued by the dead. . . . Men will think of you with revulsion; they will curse you like the plague and war; they will curse you when they curse death."[37] In America, the second generation rejects collective guilt and embraces an ethical and moral stance in the face of manifold cultural upheavals.

Collective guilt differs dramatically from collective memory. Germans born after 1940 are not responsible for the actions of their parents and grandparents. They were children and not murderers. However, they do bear a moral responsibility to remember and bear witness to their country's Holocaust past. Many young Germans went to Israel in the '50s and '60s to essentially aid the country and thereby do "penance."[38] Collective memory implies responsibility to never forget moral evil committed in the past. In a speech before the Reichstag (November 10, 1987), Wiesel drew a sharp distinction between collective guilt and collective memory. His observation deserves full citation:

> As a Jew I have never believed in collective guilt, only the guilty were guilty. Children of killers are not killers, but children. I have neither the desire nor the authority to judge today's generation for the unspeakable crimes that were committed by that of Hitler. But we may—and we must—hold it responsible not for the past but the way it remembers the past. And for what it does with the memory of the past.[39]

THE FORGOTTEN

The Forgotten is a profound meditation on the sacredness of survivor testimony and the possibility of inheriting memory. The central question is: Can memory, like blood, be transfused? Elhanan Rosenbaum is a survivor and psychotherapist living in New York City. A widower, he suffers from Alzheimer's disease and seeks to impart his memory to his son Malkiel ("God is my king," translated from the Hebrew) while there is still time. Unlike the father-son relationship in *The Fifth Son*, Elhanan and Malkiel share a close bond; father and son study Talmud together, they engage in dialogues, and Malkiel visits his father nearly every Shabbat. Wiesel paints an idealized portrait of the relationship between the two generations as each one deals with the cancer of identity which afflicts the father. (Wiesel himself, in a YouTube interview, confided that he feared losing his own memory.[40])

Elhanan, like *The Fifth Son*'s Reuven, is described as suffused by melancholy. Unlike Reuven, however, he helped people triumph over their affliction by listening. Elhanan is plagued by guilt over the wartime rape of the wife of the murderous Nylas (Hungarian Nazi) leader by his friend Itzhik. He believes that his present suffering is punishment for failing to intervene. There is much reflection on the relationship between justice and vengeance. But the novel opens with a prayer; it is Elhanan's prayer to the God of the patriarchs and it implicates the Master of the Universe in the disease of forgetting. The God of Israel is also the God of Auschwitz. This mysterious deity, "the source of all memory," knows that "to forget is to repudiate. Do not abandon me, God of my fathers," prays Elhanan, "for I have never repudiated You."[41] However, post-Shoah, the biblical deity is an implicated or, at the very least, a wounded God.

Elhanan's prayer is essentially a *Shema Yisrael* (Hear, Oh Israel) intended not for the people of Israel, but for their creator and covenantal partner:

> God of Auschwitz, know that I must remember Auschwitz. And that I must remind You of it. God of Treblinka, let the sound of that name make me, and You, tremble now and always. God of Belzec, let me, and You, weep for the victims of Belzec.[42]

Reminding God that He spared Elhanan's life in a time of danger and death so that he might testify, the survivor equates bearing witness with a sacred task. He asks, "What sort of witness would I be without my memory?"[43]

Malkiel, at his father's insistence, makes a pilgrimage to Feherfalu (White Village), Elhanan's natal Carpathian village. Professor Victoria Aarons terms such journeys "quest narratives,"[44] typical of second- and, increasingly, third-generation descendants of survivors. Recall that Ariel in *The Fifth Son* also undertook a journey of return. Physical connection to parents' birthplaces is deemed necessary to get a fuller picture of the world obliterated by the Shoah. Elhanan tells his son, "You would understand me better. You would remember more."

In Malkiel's case, it is a double-edged sword. On the one hand, it helps reify his witnessing. But, on the other hand, it also raises questions about the limits of memory transfusion. The son muses to his father:

> Of course I'll bear witness for you, but my deposition will pale before yours. What shall I do? Your life and memory are indivisible. . . . I know that whoever listens to a witness becomes one in turn . . . but we are not witnessing the same events. All I can say is, "I have heard the witness."[45]

Ultimately, however, Malkiel rejects the possibility of a memory transfusion: "Forgive me, Father. You'll have to forgive me, but I'm going to disappoint you. There is no such thing as a memory transfusion. Yours will never become mine."[46] This statement underscores two points: the unbridgeable generational gap between survivors and the second generation, and the need to understand changing paradigms in Holocaust representation.

Malkiel "acquires" Holocaust memory from three sources: taping his discussions with Elhanan, and in Feherfelu, speaking to Hershel the gravedigger and Ephraim the blind. Hershel shares the tale of the "Great Reunion," a conclave of long deceased rabbis who convene in order to help the village's Jews during the Shoah. He also tells Malkiel that he, himself, had assassinated the local leader of the antisemitic party. Ephraim the blind provides the most vivid description of inherited memory, conjuring Michelangelo's *The Creation of Adam*. "The blind man," writes Wiesel, "leaned toward Malkiel as if to inspect him; their heads touched. The old man's breath entered the young man's nostrils."[47] There is, however, a difference. Michelangelo's deity vivifies creation. Ephraim tells Malkiel to "feel the chill of his hand," and instructs him to "go home."

Consequently, bearing witness emerges as both a bond and a barrier between the generations; it is a bond in the sense of telling the tale in hopes of sensitizing listeners to the fate of the Jewish people during the Holocaust. Moreover, it is a warning to be eternally vigilant against, and to sound a warning about, the appearance of genocidal signs. It is a barrier in the sense that those who personally experienced the Shoah are ineluctably different from their children and grandchildren. Malkiel's mission is to bear witness in America, where usage of the Holocaust is becoming trivialized and distorted.

Passing the Torch of Remembrance

In 1984 Elie Wiesel delivered the keynote address at the plenary session of the First International Conference of Children of Holocaust Survivors held in New York City. Participants came from the United States, Canada, and Israel. More than 1,700 attendees heard Wiesel state that they were "guardians of the tale" of the Holocaust and—in an apparent reference to the TV miniseries *Holocaust*—should not let it be trivialized into "silly, stupid, cheap pictures on television."[48] Moreover, Wiesel charged the second generation with "[keeping] our tale alive—and sacred."[49] Do not permit its trivialization. The task of the second generation is to speak and for others to learn. Yet, acknowledging the changing generational paradigms of Holocaust representation, the second generation must seek its own voice. Recall *The Forgotten*'s Malkiel saying to his survivor father:

> Forgive me, Father, You'll have to forgive me, but I'm going to disappoint you.
> There is no such thing as a memory transfusion. Yours will never become mine.
> I can live after you and even for you, but not as you.

THE SECOND GENERATION IN AMERICA—THE CHILDREN OF JOB

Wiesel's second-generation novels opened the floodgates of Holocaust representation in America. The American second generation refrains from writing about Auschwitz itself. They were not there. Instead, their work reflects the psycho-social legacy of the Shoah in their own lives. For example, there are issues of boundaries, as frequently survivor parents cannot let go psychologically of their children; there is also the phenomenon of the impossible comparison, as a child lost in the Shoah is perfect in the parents' minds as compared to the flesh and blood post-war children. Art Spiegelman, author of the groundbreaking *Maus* volumes, told his fiancée (François) that his parents kept an enlarged photo of Richieu, their dead son, in their bedroom. Spiegelman confided that it was "spooky having sibling rivalry with a ghost." Furthermore, many survivors frequently and perhaps beyond their conscience control, dismiss, or downplay their children's disappointments by comparing them to the horrors the survivors had experienced in the Shoah. Finally, parenting the parents also emerged as a common pattern. Yet, as the late Professor William Helmreich noted, the American second generation has conflicting images of their parents. On the one hand, survivor parents "were regarded as all powerful, indestructible people who had literally made it through hell". . . On the other hand, these parents wore "ill-fitting clothes, [had] heavy accents, short height." Moreover, they were unfamiliar with American culture; "they appeared frail and weak."[50]

The American children of Job live in a time that confronts vexing questions of memory and ethnic identity. While their artistic creations are clearly autobiographical, and frequently depart from the classical notion of communal response to historical tragedy, these works continue to raise the central question of how to live Jewishly after a catastrophe. Their remedies may depart from historical norms. But their search for identity comports with traditional questioning following a disaster as well as the uncertainties of being in a new land.

Two initial 1979 studies brought the second generation into focus as a distinct group having a particular angle of vision concerning the Shoah and its meaning for American culture: Lucy Y. Steinitz and David M. Szony's edited collection, *Living After the Holocaust: Reflections by Children of Survivors Living in America*, and Helen Epstein's *Children of the Holocaust: Conversations With Sons and Daughters of the Holocaust*. These works employed images and nightmares of survivor parents in revealing how the Shoah's legacy impacted a generation that "bore the scar without the wound." These contemporary children of Job dedicated themselves to bearing witness in order to educate about the lessons and legacies of the Holocaust.[51]

Moreover, their artistic creations included several different genres. Cinematic tributes were made honoring the lives of the precious few *Hasidei Umot HaOlam*—the Righteous Among the Nations—who had saved the lives of the filmmakers' parents. One thinks here immediately of Pierre Sauvage's *Weapons of the Spirit*, which depicts the French village of Le Chambon sur Lignon, where approximately 5,000 Huguenots saved the lives of a like number of Jews, including an infant named Pierre Sauvage; and Myriam Abramowicz and Esther Hoffenberg's *As If It Were Yesterday*, which tells the story of rescue in Belgium. Space limitations prevent a full listing of the writings of the American children of Job, but among the most prominent are the short stories and novels of Thane Rosenbaum, the memoir of Helen Epstein, the graphic art of Art Spiegelman, the short stories of Lev Raphael, and the novels of Julie Salamon and Nava Semel (Israeli daughter of Shoah survivors). Critical studies include works by Alan L. Berger (*Children of Job: American Second-Generation Witnesses to the Holocaust*), Alan L. and Naomi Berger (*Second Generation Voices: Reflections by Children of Perpetrators and Survivors*), and Erin McGlothlin (*Second Generation Holocaust Literature: Legacies of Survival and Perpetration*).

There is a further paradigm shift when one turns to the work of the third generation. Here the Shoah is presented as one among several themes in a given novel or memoir. The third generation lives at a time of After Testimony. Hence their challenge is to negotiate between proximity and distance. Experientially far removed from the Holocaust, they nonetheless are existentially touched by their inheritance. They do Internet research, speak with relatives and family friends, and make pilgrimages to their grandparents' natal villages in order to find out more about their own Jewish identity. Also prominent is the rise of the graphic novel. Representative works include Daniel Mendelsohn's *The Lost: A Search for Six of the Six Million*, Nicole Kraus' *The History of Love* and *Great House*, Joseph Skibel's *A Blessing on the Moon*, Jonathan Safran Foer's *Everything Is Illuminated*, and Julie Orringer's *The Invisible Bridge*. Critical studies include Victoria Aarons' *Third-Generation Holocaust Narratives: Memory in Memoir and Fiction* and *Holocaust Graphic Narratives*, and Victoria Aarons and Alan L. Berger's (co-authors) *Third-Generation Holocaust Representation: Trauma, History, and Memory*.

Despite these and other similar works, there is cause for alarm. Holocaust denial, distortion, and trivialization continue to plague American culture. There is the increasing use of social media and its distinctly amoral stance concerning antisemitism, hate speech, and racism. In addition, among the so-called alt-right there is a prevalence of cynicism and outright Holocaust denial and employing tropes of classical antisemitism including the blood libel. Presidential re-tweeting of white national symbolism also serves to stir the cauldron of hate and divisiveness. Distortion of the Holocaust is a direct result of miseducation, but also of the failure of leaders to denounce such behavior. These are all worrying societal phenomena. Professor Alvin Rosenfeld points to this issue in his masterful 2013 book *The End of the Holocaust*. There is also the frequently used phrase "fake news" and the word "hoax" in American culture, not infrequently uttered from the highest levels of government. This serves to confuse listeners. As Wiesel frequently observed, at Auschwitz the Jews died, but the disease of antisemitism is very much alive.

Notes

1. Yosef Hayim Yerushalmi, *ZAKHOR: Jewish History and Jewish Memory*. Seattle: University of Washington Press, 1983, page 5.
2. Irving Abrahamson (editor), *Against Silence: The Voice and Vision of Elie Wiesel*. New York: Holocaust Library, 1985, volume I, page 386.
3. Yerushalmi, *ZAKHOR*, page 97.
4. Ibid., page 98.
5. Ibid.
6. Elie Wiesel and Philippe de Saint-Cheron, *Evil and Exile*. Translated by Jon Rothschild. Notre Dame: University of Notre Dame Press, 1990, page 155.
7. Ibid.
8. Elie Wiesel, *One Generation After*. Translated by Lily Edelman and Elie Wiesel. New York: Schocken Books, 1982, page 198.
9. Elie Wiesel as cited in Hillel Goldberg, "Holocaust Theology: The Survivor's Statement," *Tradition*, 20, no. 2, 1982, page 150.
10. Elie Wiesel, *The Oath*. New York: Avon Books, 1973.
11. Elie Wiesel, *The Testament*. Translated by Marion Wiesel. New York: Schocken, 1999.
12. Elie Wiesel, *The Fifth Son*. Translated by Marion Wiesel. New York: Summit Books, 1985.
13. Elie Wiesel, *The Forgotten*. Translated by Stephen Becker. New York: Summit Books, 1992.
14. Elie Wiesel, "Some Words for Children of Survivors: A Message to the Second Generation," in *The Holocaust Forty Years After*. Edited by Marcia Sachs Littell, Richard Libowitz, and Evelyn Bodek Rosen. Lewiston, NY: The Edwin Melen Press, 1989, page 7.
15. Ibid.
16. Elie Wiesel, *And the Sea Is Never Full: Memoirs, 1969*. Translated by Marion Wiesel. New York: Alfred A. Knopf, 1999, page 358.
17. Ibid.
18. Ibid.
19. See Elie Wiesel's novel *The Oath*.
20. Ibid., page 67.
21. Ibid., page 52.
22. Michael Berenbaum, *God, The Holocaust, and the Children of Israel*. West Orange: Behrman House, 1994, page 93.
23. Ibid.
24. Ibid., page 284.
25. Ibid., page 92.
26. Ibid.
27. Wiesel, *One Generation After*, page 9.

28. Elie Wiesel, *All Rivers Run to the Sea*. New York: Alfred A. Knopf, 1995, page 30.
29. Ibid.
30. Ibid.
31. Wiesel reports that Shimon Markish, the son of Peretz Markish, came to see him in Paris after the publication of *The Testament*, asking how Wiesel knew so much about his father. Wiesel replied, "When I wrote about Paltiel Kossover, I tried to admire, to love, to rehabilitate and redeem all the writers murdered by Stalin, all those who believed in the power of words, in the power of humanity." Abrahamson, *Against Silence*, page 121.
32. Ibid., page 119.
33. Wiesel, *The Testament*, page 338.
34. Wiesel, *The Fifth Son*, page 133.
35. Robert Franciosi (editor), *Elie Wiesel: Conversations*. Jackson: University Press of Mississippi, 2002, page 65.
36. Wiesel, *The Fifth Son*, pages 192–193.
37. Ibid., pages 214–215.
38. Dan Bar-On, *Legacy of Silence*. Cambridge: Harvard University Press, 1989.
39. Elie Wiesel, *From the Kingdom of Memory: Reminiscences*. New York: Summit Books, 1990, page 194.
40. YouTube interview with Charlie Rose, July 21, 1992.
41. Wiesel, *The Forgotten*, page 11.
42. Ibid.
43. Ibid., page 12.
44. Victoria Aarons, "On the Periphery: The 'Tangled Roots' of Holocaust Remembrance for the Third Generation," in Victoria Aarons and Alan L. Berger, co-authors *Third Generation Holocaust Representation: Trauma, History, and Memory*. Evanston: Northwestern University Press, 2017, page 12.
45. Wiesel, *The Forgotten*, page 148.
46. Ibid., page 147.
47. Ibid., page 196.
48. Abrahamson, *Against Silence*, page 322.
49. Cited by Alan L. Berger, *Children of Job: American Second-Generation Witnesses to the Holocaust*. Albany: SUNY Press, 1997, page 18.
50. William Helmreich, *Against All Odds: Holocaust Survivors and the Successful Lives They Made in America*. New Brunswick: Transaction Publishers, 1996, page 139.
51. For an in-depth study of the second generation and its role in educating both themselves (*tikkun atzmi*) and American culture at large (*tikkun ha-olam*) about the lessons and legacies of the Holocaust, see Berger, *Children of Job*.

CHAPTER 4

NEO-HASIDISM

A CONTEMPORARY MESSAGE

HASIDISM, A BRIEF HISTORY

Hasidism, an eighteenth-century Eastern European mystical-pietistic revival movement, emerged against a background of a Jewish world which faced external threats and internal division. Externally, there were the dangers from antisemitism with its eruptions in violence, pogroms, and hatred. This was accompanied by a frequently chaotic transition to modernity. Internally, the Jewish world of Eastern Europe was fractured and religiously stratified. There were religious virtuosi whose extreme spiritual demands did not address the needs of the majority. The historian Jacob Katz writes of this group that its religious requirements were so great that they "could not be met by the ministering angels." Rabbinic institutions for their part were too often susceptible to corruption. The religious needs of the uneducated were largely unmet. Furthermore, there was no acknowledged leader to whom they could turn. The Hasidic movement emerged out of this situation. Eighteenth-century Hasidism was founded by Israel ben Eliezer, the Ba'al Shem Tov (Besht-Master of the Good Name, 1700–1760). Wiesel described him as follows: "The hallucinated eighteenth-century visionary who, by his appeals to joy and brotherhood, by his tales too, had succeeded in bringing hope and consolation to thousands and thousands of heretofore forgotten and lost communities."[1]

He was a charismatic individual viewed by his many followers as part miracle worker and storyteller *par excellence*. Religious spontaneity, e.g., praying when moved by the spirit rather than at set times, turning somersaults and other types of ecstatic behavior characterized the first generation. The movement emphasized tales rather than philosophical explorations to spread its teachings. These tales were viewed as having the power to transform listeners. Professor Nehemia Polen writes that Hasidic tales are "endowed with ritual holiness and [have] performative power; the telling of a story creates its own sacred space."[2]

Tales had not only the power to transform but to unify their listeners. Moreover, they bound the Hasidim (followers) to their leaders (zaddikim or rebbes). Although various rebbes each had their own distinctive personality and leadership style, each was believed to be a mystic. The Hasidim believed that the voice of the Shekinah (female dimension of God) spoke from the rebbe's throat; each of the rebbes shared the goal of uplifting their adherents' spiritual life, simultaneously broadening Hasidism's teachings.

Hasidism at its inception was an oral tradition. The miracle tales and stories told by and about its founder were written only after his death. *Shivhei HaBesht* (*In Praise of the Ba'al Shem Tov*) is a collection of hagiographic tales and anecdotes emphasizing the miraculous element of the founder's life and work. Dodye Feig, Wiesel's maternal grandfather, certainly knew of this volume. He added his own considerable store of tales and Hasidic lore that he himself had heard as a follower of the Wishnitzer Rebbe (Rebbe of Wishnitz). The world portrayed in these tales was one in which a given charismatic rebbe was perceived as able to resolve his followers' distress, no matter what its origin: economic, psychological, religious, sociological, or a combination thereof. Furthermore, the Hasidic movement stressed friendship, doubtless because the Jewish people during the Shoah had such pitifully few friends, Wiesel emphasized. He described friendship as "perhaps the greatest miracle of all." The Holocaust took an enormous toll on the lives and culture of the Hasidic world. Two-thirds of European Jewry were murdered in the Shoah. Entire Hasidic dynasties were obliterated. In Auschwitz alone, a million Jews were put to death. While certainly not all of them were Hasidim, many were. Much of the European Hasidic world was destroyed in the Holocaust. The majority of the Eastern European Jews who were murdered were associated in some way or another with Hasidism and the Hasidic ethos. A vast world of Hasidic scholarship and culture vanished. Moreover, the leadership of the movement was largely exterminated. Wiesel estimated that only "three Masters survived among hundreds and hundreds."[3] Yet there were sparks of hope amid the ashes of despair. Rebbe Nachman of Bratzlav had written: "Jews, it is forbidden to despair." This admonition was written on the wall of the Warsaw Ghetto. The saved Hasidic remnant reconstituted itself in two major centers, America and Israel, absorbing elements of the host culture, except for the language, in both places, e.g., cell phones and computer literacy, while simultaneously committing to preserving and transmitting the original message, which continues to be transmitted largely in Yiddish.

Yet Wiesel noted the disparity between Hasidism in Europe and its American expression. In Europe, Hasidism "had to be in villages"; it was born in villages. It was meant for villages. Hasidism, he continued, "is not only a structure of perceptions or of melodies or of stories. It is a geography." While some streets in Brooklyn "are structured like the villages in Eastern Europe, the movement was never an urban movement, it was a village movement." The focus of this chapter is on Hasidism in America, which in point of fact transformed into Neo-Hasidism, capturing the imagination of many Americans, even those who did not live in specifically Hasidic communities.

NEO-HASIDISM IN AMERICA

Professor Arthur Green of Boston Hebrew College articulates three features of Neo-Hasidism in the broadest sense of that phrase. First, Neo-Hasidism suggests that Hasidism has a message wider than the borders of the traditional Hasidic community: Jews and others who have no intention of living Hasidic lives "might still be spiritually nourished by the stories, teachings, music of Hasidism."[4] A second sphere of influence lies in the tremendous role the image of Hasidism plays in "the religious, artistic, and intellectual creativity of non-Hasidic Jews in the twentieth century."[5] In the literary sphere, Green specifies Shmuel Yosef Agnon and Isaac Bashevis Singer. He might have also noted the work of Chaim Potok and the artist Marc Chagall. Joseph Stein, author of the play *Fiddler of the Roof*, is another candidate for inclusion. This influence, continues Green, also extends to "religious thought, music, dance, theatre, film, and painting." In the third instance, Green provides an overarching definition of Neo-Hasidism, "Hasidism for non-Hasidim."[6]

Neo-Hasidism took hold in American culture during the 1960s and 1970s. This was a period of time when fascination with "new" religious movements and psychological experimentation emphasizing joy and spiritual fulfillment combined to form the "counter-culture." This culture reacted against what it perceived as a stultifying establishment which was suffocating spontaneity of expression. The search for authentic spiritual fulfillment was widespread in America. It was a time of experimentation with the religions of the east, Buddhism and Hinduism especially, as well as new notions of religion and spirituality, sometimes connected to the use of marijuana and LSD. In the case of Hasidism, however, it was less a turn to a new religion than a *rediscovery* and re-*appropriation* of a two-century-old tradition which had ancient roots. Wiesel, as noted, was a religiously committed writer, speaker, and teacher. By dint of his witness bearing and the moral clarity of his message, he emerged as the personification of Neo-Hasidism in America.

Neo-Hasidism expanded the Lurianic kabbalah's (sixteenth-century Jewish mystical movement) understanding of the Messiah and its emphasis on utilizing every occasion as an expression of worshipping God. Rather than a particular individual Messiah figure, however, the movement believed that the zaddik, functioned as a messiah figure. (see Chapter 2.) This notion is articulated in Wiesel's novel *The Gates of the Forest*, the first of his books which was set partially in America. Gregor, the protagonist, tells his wife, Clara: "The Messiah isn't one man, Clara, he's all men. As long as there are men there will be a Messiah."[7] This is characteristic of Wiesel's two-fold emphasis on hope despite despair, and the Messianic thrust in his novels. Hasidism also stressed the notion of "worship in corporeality" (*avodah be-gashmiyyut*), which involved performing every action, even the seemingly profane, such as eating and sexual activity, with the correct "intention" (*kavvanah*), e.g., reuniting the sparks of holiness, which—according to Isaac Luria's myth of world creation—had fallen to earth, with their heavenly counterparts.

Within the American context there are many Hasidic groups ranging across the political and religious spectrum from left to right. In an essay, "Brooklyn: A New Hasidic Kingdom," Wiesel pointed to some of the American Hasidic centers. Impressionistic essays like this one help illuminate Wiesel's fiction and his philosophy. In addition to the two best known Hasidic "schools," Lubavitch and Satmar, there are "others, many others. Klausenburg and Wilsho, Bobov and Ger, Tzanz and Bratzlav, Kretchener and Koghenitz: all of Hasidic Europe is gathered"[8] in Brooklyn, especially in the borough's Williamsburg section and in Borough Park. As Polen writes: "The dynastic narrative (re)constructs the place where the dynasty began, thus giving the incumbent rebbe his identity and his mission. The postwar rebbe is largely a creation of the story of his dynasty whose shtetl no longer exists."[9] This cultural transplantation was accompanied by the re-creation of the sacred canopy within the American context. Consequently, much as in pre-Shoah Europe, the Hasidim are both isolated (in terms of location) and insulated (by dress, religion, and cultural practices) from modernity. They live according to norms of a vanished world. When a member of this community disaffiliates, it is a cause of much anguish for the one who leaves.

Unorthodox, the popular Netflix miniseries, portrays the psychic and religious upheaval caused when a young woman leaves the community. Shira Haas, the Israeli lead actress, is the granddaughter of Holocaust survivors. Tormented by the unbearable tension between faith and doubt—tradition and modernity—she flees Brooklyn and goes to Berlin. Based on a book by the Jewish-American writer Deborah Feldman, *The Scandalous Rejection of My Hasidic Roots*, the story reveals the details of her escape from an ultraorthodox religious community in Brooklyn. The popularity of the miniseries bears out Green's definition, "Hasidism for non-Hasidim."

The Lubavitch Hasidim trace their origin to Rebbe Shneur Zalman of Lyady (1745–1813), author of the *Tanya*, an important book of Hasidic philosophy and principles. He was the founder of HaBaD (*Hokmah* = wisdom, *Binah* = understanding, *Dat* = knowledge) Hasidism. Under his leadership the movement became more scholarly and analytic, tending to downplay the magical dimension. This movement originated the dynastic Lubavitch Hasidim. Their most recent leader was the late Lubavitcher Rebbe, Menachem Mendel Schneerson (1902–1994).[10] He received a degree from the University of Berlin and studied at the Sorbonne. A gifted multi-lingual leader, Schneerson was widely consulted. His followers claimed that he was the rebbe of all the Jewish people. Lubavitch is known for its popular outreach programs and for the assistance it renders to all Jews. Schneerson died childless and there has been no official successor named, although the Lubavitch empire continues its work.

Followers of Rebbe Joel Teitelbaum (1887–1979) comprise the Satmar Hasidim, a group that originated in Hungary. Teitelbaum arrived in America shortly after the end of World War II. The group rejects the precepts of modernity while embracing the past. Decidedly conservative and insular religiously, Rebbe Teitelbaum and his followers considered only his Hasidim authentically Jewish. No non-Satmar Hasidim, and certainly no secular Jews, were viewed as authentically Jewish by the Satmar group. Their disdain extends to traditional Orthodox and non-traditional Jews. Moreover, Satmar Hasidim do not recognize the legitimacy of the State of Israel since it was established by human rather than messianic hands. At times during their tense history, physical violence erupted between the Lubavitch and Satmar groups.

Concerning the American re-birth of Hasidism, Wiesel referred to the numerous Hasidic centers in America, writing, "These centers once destroyed by the executioner, have regrouped themselves at the other end of the world and are now flourishing and radiating warmth."[11] Nevertheless, the Lubavitch movement, which like the Satmar has named no successor to be their rebbe, began equating their late rebbe with the Messiah, and expected his immanent return. Some Lubavitch followers had cell phones ready so that when Schneerson reappeared as the Messiah, they could immediately contact their co-religionists. Investing the zaddik or rebbe with God-like attributes is a belief that lends itself to abuse. Although he made no public statement, Wiesel, who opposed extremism, told me that he thought Lubavitch had made a mistake in not nipping this Schneerson as Messiah equation in the bud. It is interesting to note that the decades-long leaderless situation is not without precedent. Herbert Weiner, in his fascinating book *Nine and a Half Mystics*, has a chapter on the Bratslav Hasidim, called the "dead Hasidim" since no successor to Rebbe Nachman (died 1810) has ever been designated. Sometimes there doesn't appear to be a spiritually worthy successor. However, the financial empire is sufficiently self-sustaining.

WIESEL AND NEO-HASIDISM

Wiesel, as noted earlier, had—since childhood—heard Hasidic tales from his maternal grandfather, Dodye Feig. Imbued with tales of wonder-working mystical leaders who assuaged followers' fears and provided a sense of meaning and hope amid a world in turmoil, Dodye Feig presented his grandson with a world view in which chaos was held at bay. Wiesel recalled his grandfather as "a fabulous storyteller" who "knew how to captivate an audience." Dodye Feig's tales depended not on logic but on "imagination and beauty." Wiesel continued, "I can still hear my grandfather's voice: 'There will, of course, always be someone to tell you that a certain tale cannot, could not, be objectively true. That is of no importance; an objective Hasid is not a Hasid.'"[12] At a private meeting in Israel with the son of the Wiznitzer Rebbe, Wiesel responded to the Rebbe's question about whether the stories he told were true. Wiesel responded: "In literature, Rebbe, certain things are true though they didn't happen, while others are not, even if they did." Wiesel left without receiving the Rebbe's blessing. Wiesel's response instantiates what the sociologist Peter Berger describes as a "sacred canopy" under whose shielding cover followers felt insulated against the surrounding anomic world.

Wiesel understood the importance of Hasidism in helping revitalize Judaism in one of its darkest hours. Moreover, Hasidism's outreach to the poor and uneducated made of it an inclusive movement in which friendship and hope played a significant role. Subsequently, Wiesel's commitment to tales as a way of embracing Judaism and affirming one's Jewish identity was, and is, inviolable. Tales, moreover, play a special role in Hasidism. They are a way of engaging theological truth. Wiesel wrote: "My preoccupations in literature are as much theological as they are literary, and maybe more of the former than of the latter."[13] Consequently, when Wiesel told his tales he was simultaneously conveying, interrogating, or both, certain normative theological truths. His open-ended interrogation of normative theological truths struck a responsive chord in the American psyche.

But the Hasidic movement is both the end *and the continuity* of Wiesel's religious quest. Hasidism, he attested, "contains my murdered dreams but also my efforts to bring them back to life."[14] The juxtaposition of the religious youth that he was and the survivor that he became yields an artistic and creative tension which enabled him to raise and re-raise fundamental questions about post-Holocaust Jewish identity and the validity of classical Jewish theological norms. Moreover, he confided, "the echoes of a vanished kingdom are still reverberating. And I have remained the child who loves to listen."[15] Wiesel became an increasingly influential figure in American cultural and religious life, especially after President Carter named him chairperson of the United States Holocaust Memorial Council in 1978.

Even prior to this, however, his popularity as a lecturer, especially at New York City's 92nd Street Y, his annual public lecture series at Boston University, and in Paris, made his retelling of Hasidic tales a significant cultural event. Wiesel as a witness possessed undeniable charisma and authenticity. Moreover, his prodigious literary output and his concern for social justice made him an "invaluable" public figure. He retold and recreated Hasidic tales in light of the Holocaust as a touchstone. This creative tension, as noted, informs his retellings while challenging people of various faith orientations. His tales became important for many Christian theologians and intellectuals who saw fit to interrogate their own tradition's anti-Jewish teachings. (See Chapter 2, "Wiesel's Stance on Interfaith Dialogue: Shifting Perspective.")

Furthermore, Wiesel perceived a parallel between the world out of which Hasidism emerged and contemporary American culture: each universe was searching for meaning; both felt a sense of spiritual unease; and the eighteenth, twentieth, and early twenty-first centuries longed for compassionate and enlightened leadership. In addition, the twentieth and twenty-first centuries—despite their considerable technological achievements—appeared largely closed to the possibility of faith and hope. The questions for Wiesel's advocacy of a Neo-Hasidic "remedy" for American cultural woes are: Does this remedy work? Can it be effective in a non-homogeneous culture? Will it have an impact on an increasingly secular culture? Or was this a case of culture at large "eavesdropping," as it were, on the conversation of a believer as he wrestled—like the biblical Jacob—with interrogating the deity, even as he remained inside the faith? We will return to these questions at the end of this chapter.

WIESEL'S HASIDIC TALES—THE FRENCH CONNECTION

Wiesel's recast tales also were inflected by French existentialism, which was very much part of the intellectual atmosphere when he was a student at the Sorbonne. Wiesel was especially taken by the writings of Andre Malraux and Albert Camus concerning the nature and obligation of humanity. As Professor Rosette C. Lamont observes: "For Malraux, as later for his admirer Albert Camus, the saint is not he who escapes from humanity but rather he who is willing to assume it."[16] Wiesel especially admired Camus' novel *The Plague* (*La Peste*), a novel which dealt with a pestilence carried by rats threatening the existence of a town. The rodents are driven back underground after causing many human fatalities. The townspeople celebrate. But Doctor Rieux, the physician who is the novel's hero, knows that it is just a matter of time before the rats re-appear. The novel is a parable of the eternal struggle of good against evil or, in its contemporary guise, Western civilization versus Nazism. Significantly, Camus wrote his novel in a farmhouse situated not far from the French village of Le Chambon sur Lignon, where approximately 5,000 French Huguenots saved the lives of approximately 5,000 Jews. Moreover, as Professor Lamont helpfully observes: "Both Wiesel's and Camus's healers affirm the values of life with such passionate devotion that they must be seen as champions in the combat against *Thanatos*,"[17] even if victories over death are temporary.

"Like Wiesel," writes Lamont, "Camus believed that one must never forget, that one must remain a witness." Moreover, to be a witness implies a role that transcends the temporal. Wiesel follows Camus in imagining Sisyphus happy. Just as the hero of Greek mythology was tasked with endlessly pushing a boulder up a mountain only to see it fall, and to begin anew his eternal task, Wiesel interprets Camus' message as compelling contemporaries to create hope where none exits.[18] Wiesel's Neo-Hasidism emerged, therefore, from a complex and intertwined combination of ancient Jewish texts, Hasidic tales, and existential thought, all viewed through the lens of the Holocaust. His Neo-Hasidic tales are larger than the sum of their parts.

WIESEL'S NEO-HASIDIC TALES

Souls on Fire, which he dedicates to his grandfather and his father, refers both to the Hasidic masters whose stories he retells and, equally important, to his own soul, which is aflame to bear witness on behalf of the dead and for the living. It is worth recalling the book's dedication in full:

> My father, an enlightened spirit, believed
> In man.
> My grandfather, a fervent Hasid, believed
> In God.
> The one taught me to speak, the other to sing.
> Both loved stories.
> And when I tell mine, I hear their voices.

Whispering from beyond the silenced storm,
They are what links the survivor to their memory.

I will return to this point shortly.

The book, winner of the Prix Bordin de l'Academie Française, became a type of bible for American culture in the early '70s. Moreover, Professor Alan Rosen terms the book "not only significant in its own right, but also one that marked a watershed in Elie Wiesel's career." The volume "broke new ground" because it was the "first to delve into an entire swath of Jewish tradition."[19] Wiesel subsequently wrote other volumes on Hasidism, including *Four Hasidic Masters and Their Struggle Against Melancholy*, and *Somewhere a Master: Further Hasidic Portraits and Legends*. Beginning with the Ba'al Shem Tov, the movement's founder, Wiesel relays what he perceives as the essential message of each of the eight Hasidic leaders and their selected followers that he explores in the book.

While each of the masters has a distinctive style, Wiesel's creative recounting unites their various attempts to bring spiritual succor to their followers. The resulting literary portraits help readers to a two-fold understanding: why Wiesel returns to these figures and how the world of eighteenth-century Hasidism can address contemporary existential issues. Wiesel himself commented on the significance of the volume's title:

> Why [is the book titled] *Souls on Fire*: Because theirs [the souls of the Hasidic masters] were on fire? Yes. But even more so because they possessed the rare ability of inspiring Others and giving . . . something that is lacking today: fervor.[20]

However, Wiesel's literary re-creation of Hasidism is, strictly speaking, neither an historical account of the movement nor a scholarly analysis. It is, rather, an exquisite portrayal of Neo-Hasidism as "Hasidism for non-Hasidim." Green, again, observes that Wiesel "offers the first significant retelling of the story of Hasidism after the Holocaust."[21] Yet the Shoah is always part of the tale. Discussing the Kotzker Rebbe (Menachem Mendel of Kotzk, 1787–1859), Wiesel offers several hypotheses for the many legends surrounding the question of why the Rebbe embraced solitude for the last two decades of his life. To cite but one of them, the Kotzker apparently blasphemes by exclaiming there is neither judge nor justice in Jewish history. Moreover, he extinguishes the Shabbat candles prior to the conclusion of Shabbat, thereby violating the Sabbath laws. Afterward, he retreats to his room where he remains in seclusion for 20 years until his death. Wiesel hypothesizes: "Could he have foreseen that one hundred years after his retreat another fire would set the continent ablaze, and that its first victims would be Jewish men and women abandoned by God and by all mankind?"[22] In another eighteenth-century legend, two brothers, Reb Zusia and Reb Elimelekh, arrive in a small village near Cracow. They intended to stay overnight; however they felt compelled to leave. The name of the village: Auschwitz.

In the American context, five names, in addition to Wiesel, stand out in the popularization of Neo-Hasidism: Martin Buber; Shlomo Carlebach; Zalman Schächter-Shalomi; Menachem Mendel Schneerson, the Lubavitcher Rebbe; and Abraham Joshua Heschel. A professor of Jewish mysticism and social ethics at the Jewish Theological Seminary of America, Heschel himself was a mystic who marched with Dr. Martin Luther King in Selma. Commenting on this experience, Heschel claimed that he was praying with his legs. Reverend King termed Heschel "Father Abraham." Heschel's poetic writings and his commitment to social justice—he was among the earliest figures to advocate for Russian Jewry—gained popularity in American culture with both the Jewish and Christian communities. (See Chapter 5 for more on Heschel.)

Buber was an early popularizer of Hasidic tales, although not a Hasid himself. As Green notes, however, Buber relied on Hasidic tales, and not on the movement's "rather abstruse" sermons.[23] Moreover, the tales comported better with Buber's "existential reading" of Hasidism, which stressed "human relationships," especially the "deep soul-bonds between rebbe and disciple." Doubtless this understanding fed naturally into Buber's celebrated concept of the "I-Thou" relationship, which for the European-born social philosopher was a metaphor for the human relationship with God. Moreover, Buber, with his white beard and exotic accent, became an instantly recognizable figure on the American cultural scene.

Shlomo Carlebach, known as the "singing rabbi," sought to teach a simple faith which, coupled with his music, frequently resulted in a type of revival meeting atmosphere. Less scholarly than Buber, his emphasis was on joy, fellowship, and enthusiasm. Carlebach traversed America giving concerts and providing what he felt was an authentic Hasidic milieu for his many listeners. After his passing, Carlebach's daughter Neshama assumed her father's mantle and is a popular singer for American Jewish audiences.

Schächter-Shalomi, like Carlebach, stressed the tales of Hasidism's early masters. As Green emphasizes, these tales and teachings supplanted Talmud study or "strict attention to halachic detail."[24] Furthermore, Schächter-Shalomi's insistence on obliterating restrictions and crossing borders between "men's and women's realms, between Jew and Gentile, between old customs and new innovations" reflect the "impact of 1960s new-age religions." Moreover, it nicely facilitated his interest in dialoguing with other, especially non-Western, faiths.

Rebbe Menachem Mendel Schneerson was the last Lubavitch leader. He had studied math, physics, and philosophy at the University of Berlin, as well as at the Sorbonne in the 1920s and 1930s. Schneerson was also a Talmud scholar and was considered a religious genius. People from all walks of life sought his advice on many matters, not only faith issues. Lubavitch is the most widely recognized Hasidic group in America and the one whose outreach programs touch the lives of hundreds of thousands of Jews, both in America and abroad, regardless of their denominational affiliation or even if they are unaffiliated with any synagogue. The Lubavitcher Rebbe was known for his love of the Jewish people, his visage appeared on calendars, and the faithful hung his photo in their homes. His photograph also is displayed in many kosher restaurants. Schneerson's grave site is considered a holy place and is referred to by many as the "American Western Wall." The late Rebbe was also involved in Wiesel's personal life, having given his blessing to Marion and Elie Wiesel's newborn son, Elisha. In addition, Schneerson urged Wiesel to write a biography of Schneur Zalman of Lyady.

Wiesel's fictional dialogue with Rebbe Schneerson, which appears in the former's novel *The Gates of the Forest* ("winter section"), marks a turning point in the author's own understanding of the role of God during the Shoah. Gregor, the novel's protagonist, attends a Hasidic *farbrengin* (gathering). There he and the Rebbe discuss the relationship between God and the Holocaust. The Rebbe contends that "Auschwitz proves that nothing has changed, that the primeval war goes on. Man is capable of love and hate, murder and sacrifice. He is Abraham and Isaac together. God himself hasn't changed."[25] Gregor (a Wieselian figure) angrily asks the holy man, "After what happened to us, how can you believe in God?" "With an understanding smile on his lips," writes Wiesel, the Rebbe answered, "How can you *not* believe in God after what has happened?" Elsewhere, Wiesel writes, "Well, that was a turning point in my writing, that simple dialogue."[26] I accepted the Rebbe's response not as an answer, but as a question—one more question. Wiesel sent Rebbe Schneerson copies of his published books in French, on which the Rebbe would read and comment.

Wiesel, unlike Carlebach or Schächter-Shalomi, *did not* seek to become a leader of the Neo-Hasidic movement. And unlike Buber, his love was for individual Jews and for Judaism. Buber was not by temperament either a Hasid or a religiously observant Jew (his wife, Paula, was a Catholic convert to Judaism). Moreover, as Green notes, Wiesel was less interested in the Hasidic community that fascinated Buber. Rather, attests Green, Wiesel's "own lonely postwar years of personal quest and struggle . . . in the Parisian intellectual milieu . . . are present in the lives of Hasidic masters as he presents them."[27] Wiesel's Neo-Hasidism, attests Green, "existed mainly in his books and his multiple lecture series on Hasidic masters."

In addition, Wiesel himself was a charismatic figure who spoke with the moral authority of a witness. Wiesel, after the death of Abraham Joshua Heschel, increasingly became a "rebbe figure" for American Jewry. I personally have been at receptions for Wiesel and know that he always made time to speak with any Hasid who requested a private conversation.

Green asserts that Wiesel was instrumental in helping American and even world Jewry do two important things: universalize the Holocaust survivors' message, thereby speaking up for others who had been victimized by tyrannical political regimes, and, even more importantly, help lead in healing the Holocaust wound. I would add a third thing. Wiesel aided in helping develop a positive Jewish identity and led in the fight against despair in spite of much empirical evidence that justifies that feeling. In Camus' aphorism, in a world without hope, it is your task to create hope.

Souls on Fire was Elie Wiesel's first book devoted solely to Hasidism and its contemporary message. Ultimately there would be two other volumes plus selected sketches in additional novels, not to mention countless public lectures, devoted to the Hasidic ethos. In a 1971 letter to James H. Silverman, his then editor at Random House, Wiesel stated four reasons why in his view Hasidism had become increasingly popular. First, he stressed "the importance and sacredness of man and what makes him human."[28] Second, there is an affinity between the eighteenth century and our own times. Third, Hasidism stresses the element of beauty in Judaism. The Hasidic movement taught that Judaism is not only religion, philosophy, or ethical principles; it is also a work of art which contains beauty. Most importantly, Wiesel attested, Hasidic teachings are transmitted in tales rather than in "abstract formulas" or "rigid systems."[29] Consequently, it is not possible to be a theoretical Hasid. Hasidism is rather a way of life which informs all of an individual's attitudes, perspectives, and choices.

Conflating what he views as Hasidism's central message and influenced by the writings of Camus, Wiesel stressed Hasidism's emphasis on friendship—what he termed the greatest miracle—and lessening the solitude of individuals. Interpreting the role of the Besht, Hasidism's founder, Wiesel writes: "He simply appeared wherever he, or someone like him, was necessary, wherever utterly alone men and women, on the brink of despair, needed a sign, a messenger"[30] Furthermore, Wiesel was willing to, in the felicitous phrase of Donielle Hartman, "put God second," as it were. Beshtian Hasidism, in Wiesel's retelling, stresses that "it is in man that God must be loved, because the love of God goes through the love of man."[31] To ignore human need in order to serve God, in Wiesel's view, is to do a disservice to both God and humanity.

Wiesel self-identified as a storyteller "who transmits what was given to him, as faithfully as possible, yet *lending it his own voice and intonation and sometimes his wonder or simply: his fervor.*"[32] Thus, Wiesel's account of Hasidism is both enhanced and possibly idealized by his personal experience. His stated goal was to "bring back to life" some of the characters that peopled his childhood universe. He also speculated about the renewed interest in (Neo-)Hasidism in America. It is, he opined, possible that contemporary humans feel guilty. The death of the European Hasidic world may weigh on contemporary conscience. But Wiesel was, above all else, a religious man (*homo religious*) for whom prayer was essential. Consequently, he suggested that contemporary humanity is "moved and troubled" by the Hasidic message, whose loss is somehow related to humanity's "inability to believe and persevere." And yet, to employ Wiesel's signature phrase, his own Hasidic fervor was tempered by what had been lost. He wrote:

> Of all these people [at the Hasidic *farbrengen*], I alone know that this miraculous survival is almost a sham: the Hasidic movement has lost more than it dares admit even to itself. We are after all in Brooklyn and not in Sighet or Wiznitz.[33]

Wiesel drew certain parallels between the world which Hasidism confronted and the America of the 1970s. America at the time of the appearance of *Souls on Fire* was a country ill at ease. Economically, there was stagflation and unemployment. The price of gas had quadrupled from 25 cents a gallon to one dollar. Interest on mortgages ranged from 14% to 18%. The Watergate scandal and the resignation of President Richard M. Nixon led to a widespread mood of distrust of the government. Consequently, Wiesel appeared as a literary, moral, and theological pied piper whose message was one of hope as opposed to despair, meaning in contrast to purposelessness, and friendship instead of alienation. In his view Hasidic tales retold and reworked in light of the Holocaust could provide a cultural lifeline for contemporary times. But Wiesel's Hasidic focus had universal resonance. He intended to validate the Jewish view of the intrinsic value of human life as opposed to Nazism's specific intention to murder every Jewish person. Nazism had installed death and killing at the center of its perverted universe. Wiesel wrote instead to attest to the sacredness of life and the salvific nature of friendship in a world that is too often indifferent.

Wiesel's Hasidic message found great reverberation in American culture for several reasons. There was, in the first instance, the impact of the man himself. In the manner of Marshall McLuhan's dictum "The medium is the message," Wiesel not only told Hasidic tales, he embodied their essence. His background as a Holocaust survivor, his voice, and his

European accent all combined to render him a charismatic figure in a time when American culture was sorely lacking in this area. Wiesel's Hasidic tales constituted what McLuhan termed "hot" media, which means that the consumer does not need to exert much effort in filling in the details to determine the media's meaning. When the world is in turmoil, one seeks a better way. Hasidism held out a singular vision which transcended an either/or approach. Instead, Hasidism and Wiesel embraced paradox. Wiesel liked to cite Reb Mendel from the School of Worke and its dual emphasis on friendship and silence. He told his disciples to follow three principles: "Learn how to kneel and stand erect; to dance and remain motionless; to shout and be silent—all at the same time."[34]

As a mystic, Wiesel was fond of embracing paradox as a way to seek hope in spite of massive evidence to the contrary. This is one meaning of his phrase "And yet," which keeps the conversation alive and offers a glimmer of light in an otherwise grim world. He was also fond of citing Reb Nahman of Bratzlav, great-grandson of Hasidism's founder, Besht, who attested, "There is nothing as whole as a broken heart." For Nahman, as for Wiesel, the ability to hope even when the worst is known stimulates messianic yearning and imbues life with a purpose. Nahman, arguably the greatest storyteller in Hasidism, and a precursor of the enigmatic Franz Kafka, urged that his tales be made into prayers. Wiesel reversed this by contending that his prayers should be made into tales. In either case, Wiesel's prayers and Nahman's tales bear potentially salvific resonance.

Parallels Between Eighteenth-Century Europe and Post-War America

Wiesel, as previously noted, viewed the eighteenth and twentieth centuries, and with alarming speed the twenty-first century, as existentially similar. For all three time periods the world is in disarray. If one were to choose artistic representation of the surreal environment, one would think of Salvador Dali, Franz Kafka, Pablo Picasso, Igor Stravinsky, Marc Chagall, and Gustav Mahler. Moreover, each century experienced a leadership crisis which caused people to feel both despair and rage. So-called alternative facts all too frequently under the Trump administration became a synonym for lying. Furthermore, each period is characterized by a search for meaning in the face of meaninglessness.

The post-Holocaust and post-modern ethos of anomie and ethical and moral disjunction left many wandering in a spiritual wilderness. Wiesel emerged as the proponent of a basic principle of Hasidic teaching: "Our love for our fellow man must resemble God's; it must aspire to be infinite."[35] Universalizing the principle of *Ahavat Ysrael* (Love of the Jewish People),

Wiesel's Neo-Hasidic point of view enabled him to contend that the more Jewish he was, the more he could reach out to his fellow human being regardless of their religious orientation. Citing the Hasidic Zaddik Meir of Premshlan (1780–1850) as his example of helping those in desperate need, Wiesel extrapolated the following lesson: "When there are people going hungry, they must come first; their well-being must take precedence over all ideals—no, their well-being must become our ideal. The Messiah can wait and he should."

Wiesel turned to the School of Worke to buttress his contention. "In Worke," he wrote, the stress was on the humanist implications of Hasidism, and "friendship was as important as study." Professor Frederick Downing observes that "the theme [Wiesel] carries with him for a lifetime . . . is that of a sense of separation and abandonment."[36] It is therefore not surprising that in his retellings of the Hasidic world, he stresses friendship, which, as we have seen, he terms the greatest miracle of all. In the Afterword to *Somewhere a Master: Further Hasidic Portraits and Legends*, Wiesel writes: "Friendship, *Dibuk-haverim*, is a key word in the Hasidic vocabulary."[37] Wiesel carries this theme further in observing: "What was the Hasidic movement in its origins if not a protest against solitude?" For Wiesel, the messages of the rebbes and zaddikim constituted an invitation to contemporary people to find a teacher or master. For many, Wiesel himself as an unparalleled storyteller functioned as this master. Instilling hope in a world which frequently appears to have learned no lessons from the Shoah about antisemitism, racism, and the propensity for evil, Wiesel emerged as a Sisyphus figure, condemned to forever push the boulder of hope up a mountain of despair only to witness it roll down again. The task is eternal.

Reading Wiesel's interpretive portraits of the Hasidic masters, one thing becomes clear: *his descriptions are frequently self-portraits*. Summing up the Kotzker Rebbe's life, Wiesel writes, "One senses . . . the obsessions and conflicts of a man struggling with what negates yet attracts him, with what exalts yet mows him down: death, faith and the absolute."[38] Is this not Wiesel the survivor speaking? The person who commented, "Ever since Auschwitz I have been trying to find an occupation for God"? I add here that in response to my question of whether he had found such an occupation for the deity, Wiesel replied, "yes, but He does not listen."

Here are other examples. Wiesel asked, what was the key idea of the School of Pshiskhe? He then referred to Yaakov Yitzhak (1776–1813), known as the "Jew," Levi Yitzhak (1740–1809), and Rebbe Bunam (1762–1827). The "Jew" meant *man* when he spoke of the Jew. Rebbe Bunam meant *the Jew* when he spoke of man. This merges with Wiesel's attestation of the relationship between the particular and the universal.

Reflecting on the key idea of the School of Pshiskhe, and his own immersion in existential thought, Wiesel believed that both Hasidic leaders wished man to believe that he could draw strength from the despair that is part of the human condition. Wiesel writes, "Since man is alone, he helps his fellow man and thereby breaks his own solitude."[39] Aphoristically, Wiesel contended that one may be Jewish with God or against God, but never without God. Here he echoed the example of Levi Yitzhak of Berditchev, who protested God's injustice while remaining firmly within the Jewish tradition. Moreover, Wiesel also embraced Rebbe Nachman of Bratzlav's teaching, which forbade Jews to despair, in spite of having every reason to do so. Wiesel was of course very conscious of the debt he owed Hasidism. He wrote:

> Sometimes consciously, sometimes not, I have incorporated a song, a suite, an obsession of [the Hasidic masters] into my own fables and legends. For me, the echoes of a vanished kingdom are still reverberating. And I have remained the child who loves to listen.[40]

One gets the sense that in retelling these tales, Wiesel was simultaneously listening as well as telling.

ELIE WIESEL—A SOUL ON FIRE

Wiesel's life was intimately tied to the notion of fire. But as the French philosopher Gaston Bachelard wrote in his important book *The Psychoanalysis of Fire*, fire contains opposing values of good and evil;[41] fire has both a life-threatening and life-sustaining capacity. It can cook the food we eat, and it can consume our flesh. Wiesel's canonical memoir *Night*, a text which describes the anti-Exodus experience of Sighet's Jews (they had been deported during Passover), contains many defining instances of fire as life-destroying. In the transport to Auschwitz, Mrs. Schächter,

> a woman in her fifties and her ten-year-old son crouched in a corner. She had gone mad when her husband and two older sons had accidentally been deported. She utters a hallucinatory scream, "Fire! I see a fire! I see a fire." "Look!" she continues, "Look at this fire! This terrible fire! Have mercy on me!" But only darkness surrounded the train.[42]

Wiesel reports that the woman's husband had been taken on an earlier transport and that she had suffered a nervous breakdown. She was bound and gagged. Wiesel reports that her screams "tore us apart." Once in Birkenau, however, the flames were no longer illusory. This time Sighet's Jews "saw flames rising from a tall chimney into a black sky." Moreover, Wiesel writes, "In the air, the smell of burning flesh. . . . We had arrived. In

Birkenau."[43] It was part of the Auschwitz complex, located approximately 3.5 kilometers from the main camp (Stammlager) of Auschwitz.

Wiesel's pre-Holocaust world, firmly anchored in traditional Jewish beliefs about God protecting the Jewish people and the efficacy of prayer itself, was literally consumed by fire. Wiesel writes: "The student of Talmud, the child that I was, had been consumed by the flames. All that was left was a shape that resembled me. My soul had been invaded—and devoured— by a black flame."[44] Wiesel observed that fire not only destroyed human beings physically. "The image of man was also obliterated in Auschwitz."

But fire also serves, as Rosen puts it, "the essence of serving God passionately, totally, unreservedly."[45] It was in part to restore the human image that Wiesel turned to Hasidism and its life-affirming message. Wiesel wrote to his editor at Random House explaining why he chose the title *Souls on Fire*:

> Because theirs were on fire? Yes. But even more so because they possessed the rare ability of inspiring others and giving them more than excitement, more than hope, more than comfort; they gave their followers something that is lacking today: fervor.[46]

Moreover, Wiesel saw the tales of the Hasidic masters as a "bridge between then and now . . . between the joy of then and the anxiety of today." Wiesel was not the first Jewish thinker to associate "fire" in Judaism with devotion to God. This phenomenon finds expression as far back as the Talmud. However, in Hasidism, as Rosen notes, Shneur Zalman, founder of Lubavitch Hasidism (died 1813), "describes the love born of the profound contemplation of God's greatness as a 'burning in his heart like a flame, like fiery flashes.'"[47] Fervor remains the defining characteristic of the Hasidic masters. "It is said of anyone who came to see Rebbe Bunam of Pshiske," writes Wiesel, "that his soul caught on fire."[48] Similarly, the Holy Seer of Lublin attested "absence of fire, absence of passion leads to indifference and resignation—in other words to death."[49]

WIESEL'S HASIDIC TALES: CURE OF THE SELF, CURE OF SOCIETAL ILLS

Wiesel, in America, shared his Hasidic fervor as a way of personally beginning anew in light of the Shoah, and as a cure for societal malaise. We must not, however, take the word "cure" in its literal sense. The Holocaust is not like a physical illness from which one recovers and is pronounced cured. It is rather the case that Auschwitz and its legacy, while definitely bearing physical consequences, inflict a heavy psycho-social toll. Individuals need to work through their traumatic legacy. As William Helmreich notes in his insightful book *Against All Odds: Holocaust Survivors and the Successful Lives They Made in America*, some survivors in America led successful lives, contributing to American and Jewish culture. But each survivor carried the psychic toll of Auschwitz on her or his back. Wiesel in America found himself in a totally different cultural and religious ambience than either pre-war Sighet or post-war Paris. He strode on an invisible bridge which simultaneously led him away from and back to his pre-Holocaust beliefs.

Concerning the possibility of a repair of the self (*tikkun atzmi*) insofar as this is possible after the horrors of the Holocaust, Wiesel instinctively turned to the world of Hasidism and its boundless tales. He writes:

> In retelling these tales, I realize once more that I owe them much. Consciously or not,
> I have incorporated a song, an echo, a word of theirs in my own legends and fables. I have
> Remained, in a vanished kingdom, a child who loves to listen.
> More than ever, we, today, need their faith, their fervor; more than ever, we today, need to imagine them [the Hasidic masters] helping, caring—living.[50]

Repairing of the world requires, even while transcending, repairing of the self. Wiesel had lived in two diametrically opposed worlds. A God-intoxicated youth in Sighet, he studied religious and mystical Jewish texts, which guided him to live under the sheltering wings of a sacred canopy where life had meaning, and the cosmos was one of order in which life was valued. He had also experienced the anti-world of Nazi death camps. There human life, especially Jewish life, was without intrinsic value or meaning. Existence in the death camps was anomic, cruel, and without hope. Confronted by these two different worlds, Wiesel needed to search for a purpose that took both into account. He had seen how society could be transformed into a vast kingdom of death. Consequently, he attested that bearing witness was vital in order that his past (the Holocaust) did not become humanity's future.

America in the late '60s and early '70s was a country in turmoil. As noted earlier, there was widespread search for meaning amid a drift toward anomie. This meaning assumed a variety of guises: Asian religions, cults, spiritualism, psychological "cures" such as EST, and the use of hallucinogens, among others. Politically there was great skepticism. As an aside, Wiesel, on more than one occasion, noting the deterioration of America's cities, reminded listeners that the biblical Cain—slayer of his brother Abel—was the founder of cities. Wiesel believed that he had a crucial message for America and beyond this country's shores. As a storyteller, "he only tries to wrest from death certain prayers, certain faces, by appealing to the imagination and the nostalgia that make man listen when his story is told." Wiesel viewed with great alarm the manifold societal crises which engulfed contemporary society. He was convinced that "more than ever, we, today, need their [Hasidic masters] faith, their fervor."[51] One can only shudder when contemplating—with horror— how Wiesel would feel when confronting the dystopian universe ushered in by the results of the 2016 presidential election.

Wiesel's concern over the direction of the contemporary world was perhaps most clearly revealed by the controversy surrounding the 1983 film *The Day After*. This film dramatized the nuclear threat which hung, and continues to hang, over the world like a sword of Damocles. Commentators from a variety of fields, military, diplomatic, and political, were invited to appear on Ted Koppel's *Viewpoint* program to offer opinions following the film. Wiesel was asked to offer a humanities perspective. As Downing notes, Wiesel's response was "to admit fear for the human species." Wiesel continued, perhaps, he theorized, "the world has turned Jewish." What had earlier happened to the Jewish people was now a universal threat. The Jewish people in this view serve as the proverbial canary in the coal mine. Wiesel postulated that humanity itself may cease to exist. As Downing writes, for Wiesel the only remedy to possibly save mankind was through memory and education, not through a weapons program.[52] The Hasidic view about the sacrality of human existence and the preciousness of life itself increasingly appears in abeyance.

WIESEL'S NEO-HASIDISM REVISITED

Clearly, for Wiesel Hasidism and Hasidic tales were paradigmatic; they enable one to live in a world of meaning, safeguarded under a sacred canopy which helps keep chaos at bay. This is not to assert that the Hasidic masters were not themselves at times beset by melancholy or despair. Occasionally they were (see *Four Hasidic Masters and Their Struggle Against Melancholy*). In a self-revealing question, Wiesel asked, "How did they manage to keep their faith intact?" Wiesel, the master storyteller, of course had his own moments of despair. The world, he once told me, has learned nothing. He also had his own very real problems with God. But his quarrels, doubts, and interrogations of the divine were all expressed from *within* the tradition. Stressing questions rather than answers enabled him to continue. In Sighet, Moishe the Beadle, his teacher of kabbalah (Jewish mysticism), told the youth that man comes closer to God through the questions he asks Him. As noted, the word question has two crucial connotations; it contains the word quest, and in Hebrew *she'elah* contains El—a name of God. The dialogue between man and God and between Hasid and rebbe embraces questions and encourages hope.

Has Wiesel presented an idealized portrait of the Hasidic masters and the healing power of tales? Perhaps. He confessed, "I glorify them."[53] "My purpose was not to create a scholarly work of critical analysis. The only role that suits [me] is—storyteller who transmits what was given to him, as faithfully as possible, yet lending it [my] own voice and intonations and sometimes [my] fervor."[54] But he has done so in the service of a greater good, the pursuit of a mending of the self and the potential healing of society. Wiesel's Neo-Hasidism provided both a potential remedy for societal ills and a modality by which individuals beset by cultural and theological doubt can move forward in an uncertain and fraught time. Moreover, beyond the political, Wiesel's Neo-Hasidic universe was concerned with existential questions and truths. These questions are eternal and provide guidelines by which people, both Jews and non-Jews, can seek to live their lives under a sacred canopy, which is a guard against the exigencies of the moment. Far from being whimsical or selfish, this canopy is a beacon of light in a world which ebbs and flows according to the fleeting and ever-changing vicissitudes of the moment. This is especially the case in America during a "crazy-making" time where cultural and political distractions abound.

The American political climate is fraught. Various and competing solutions are offered by different political, religious, and psychological gurus and panacea mongers. Amid this turmoil, Wiesel offered what he believed a means to live a fuller, happier, and fulfilling life by reaching out to God, by reaching out to one's fellow human beings, and by embracing memory, even while acknowledging that despair is real, but can be surmounted. He was well aware of the moral responsibility of both individuals and national governments. He was also keenly aware of the perversion of religion by fanaticism and the radical assault on truth and morality. His bedrock message concerned the sacredness of human life and the beauty of friendship. His Neo-Hasidic message provides Americans with an alternative to discord and rancor. In their stead stands recognition that the road to God does indeed require reaching out to one's fellow human beings.

A central feature of Wiesel's Neo-Hasidic writings and public lectures is an affirmation of the Jewish view of the sacred worth of human life. This stands in the sharpest contrast to the Nazi attempt to obliterate all Jewish, and any other, life they deemed superfluous, dangerous, or a menace to the Third Reich. Neo-Hasidism in this instance embraces an ethic of the highest moral standard. These two world views—Jewish life affirming and National Socialism's global murder campaign—could not long co-exist. Wiesel viewed his mission as the articulation of the fundamental preciousness of life. His "yes" to life emerged in the face of the radical "no" which issued from the death camps. Memory, friendship, and reasons for hope all coalesce in Wiesel's post-Shoah embrace of Neo-Hasidism.

Chapter 5 discusses how Wiesel's defiant activism led to his fight for social justice.

NOTES

1. Elie Wiesel, "Brooklyn: A New Hasidic Kingdom." Translated by Marion Wiesel. Elie Wiesel Collection. Gottlieb Archive. Mugar Library. Boston: Boston University Press, 1975, page 1.
2. Nehemia Polen, "Yearning for Sacred Place: Wiesel's Hasidic Tales and Postwar Hasidism," in *Elie Wiesel: Jewish, Literary, and Moral Perspectives*. Edited by Steven T. Katz and Alan Rosen. Bloomington: Indiana University Press, 2013, pages 69–70.
3. Roger Lipsey, "We Are All Witnesses: An Interview with Elie Wiesel," *Parabola*, X, no. 2, "Exile," Summer 1975, page 10.
4. Arthur Green, "Wiesel in the Context of Neo-Hasidism," in *Elie Wiesel: Jewish, Literary, and Moral Perspectives*. Edited by Steven T. Katz and Alan Rosen. Bloomington: Indiana University Press, 2013, page 51.
5. Ibid.
6. Ibid.
7. Elie Wiesel, *The Gates of the Forest*. Translated by Frances Frenaye. New York: Schocken Books, page 225.
8. Wiesel, "Brooklyn: A New Hasidic Kingdom," page 12.
9. Polen, "Yearning for Sacred Place," page 72.
10. By including Rebbes Menachem Mendel Schneerson and Joel Teitelbaum in this chapter, I by no means wish to suggest they illustrate Neo-Hasidism. Quite the reverse is this case. Their followers are committed by reason of faith and duration to their respective leaders. They live according to the norms of a vanished world, remaining conservative and religiously insular, which involves following the zaddik or rebbe.
11. Wiesel, "Brooklyn: A New Hasidic Kingdom," page 12.
12. Elise Wiesel, *Souls on Fire: Portraits and Legends of Hasidic Masters*. Translated by Marion Wiesel. New York: Random House, 1972, page 7.
13. Irving Abrahamson (editor), *Against Silence: The Voice and Vision of Elie Wiesel*. New York: Holocaust Library, 1985, volume II, page 139.
14. Elie Wiesel, *And the Sea Is Never Full: Memoirs, 1969*. Translated by Marion Wiesel. New York: Knopf, 1999, page 28.
15. Elie Wiesel, *Somewhere a Master: Further Hasidic Portraits and Legends*. Translated by Marion Wiesel. New York: Simon & Schuster, Touchstone Books, 1993, page 205.
16. Rosette C. Lamont, "Elie Wiesel: In Search of a Tongue," in *Confronting the Holocaust: The Impact of Elie Wiesel*. Edited by Alvin H. Rosenfeld and Irving Greenberg. Bloomington: Indiana University Press, 1978, page 87.
17. Ibid., page 95.
18. Based on Green, Op. Cit., page 55.
19. Alan Rosen, "Capturing the Fire, Envisioning the Redemption," in *Elie Wiesel: Teacher, Mentor and Friend*. Edited by Alan L Berger. Eugene, OR: Cascade Books, 2018, page 51.
20. Irving Abrahamson (editor), *Against Silence: The Voice and Vision of Elie Wiesel*. New York: Holocaust Library, 1985, volume III, page 79.
21. Green, "Wiesel in the Context of Neo-Hasidism," page 54.
22. Wiesel, *Souls*, page 254.
23. Green, "Wiesel in the Context of Neo-Hasidism," page 53.
24. Ibid., page 56.
25. Wiesel, *The Gates of the Forest*, 1996 page 194.

26. Abrahamson, *Against Silence: The Voice and Vision of Elie Wiesel*, volume III, page 63.
27. Green, "Wiesel in the Context of Neo-Hasidism," page 55.
28. Abrahamson, *Against Silence: The Voice and Vision of Elie Wiesel*, volume III, page 77.
29. Ibid., page 78.
30. Wiesel, *Souls*, page 19.
31. Ibid., page 31.
32. Ibid., page 255. Emphasis in original.
33. Wiesel, "Brooklyn: A New Hasidic Kingdom," page 15.
34. Wiesel, *Somewhere a Master*, page 198.
35. Ibid., page 65.
36. Frederick L. Downing, *Elie Wiesel: A Religious Biography*. Macon, GA: Mercer University Press, 2008, page 34.
37. Wiesel, *Somewhere a Master*, page 203.
38. Ibid.
39. Wiesel, *Souls*, page 223.
40. Wiesel, *Somewhere a Master*, page 205.
41. Gaston Bachelard, *The Psychoanalysis of Fire*. Boston: Beacon Press, 1964, chapter 1.
42. Elie Wiesel, *Night*. Translated by Marion Wiesel. New York: Hill and Wang, 2006, page 27.
43. Birkenau was part of the Auschwitz complex and was located approximately 3.5 kilometers from the main campus (Stammlager) of Auschwitz.
44. Wiesel, *Night*, page 37.
45. Rosen, "Capturing the Fire, Envisioning the Redemption," page 53.
46. Abrahamson, *Against Silence: The Voice and Vision of Elie Wiesel*, volume III, page 79.
47. Rosen, "Capturing the Fire, Envisioning the Redemption," page 54.
48. Abrahamson, *Against Silence: The Voice and Vision of Elie Wiesel*, volume III, page 84.
49. Elie Wiesel, *Four Hasidic Masters*. South Bend: Notre Dame University Press, 1978, page 81.
50. Ibid., page 205.
51. Wiesel, *Somewhere a Master,* page 205.
52. Downing, *Elie Wiesel: A Religious Biography*, page 231.
53. Wiesel, *Somewhere a Master*, page 8.
54. Wiesel, *Souls*, page 255.

HUMAN RIGHTS

Elie Wiesel waged a ceaseless struggle for justice. As an acclaimed author, he viewed writing as the art of correcting injustice. Whether his focus was on local or international efforts, the dignity of individual lives was his standard of moral judgment. From revulsion at the "whites only" drinking fountains in the American South to the unjust apartheid regime in South Africa, the Noble Peace laureate called out those who oppressed human rights. Moreover, Wiesel's concern was unrelenting even though its triumph was far from certain. "There may be times," he wrote, "when we are powerless to prevent injustice, but there must never be a time when we fail to protest."[1]

The arc of Wiesel's human rights concern was high and wide. For example, he wrote about, spoke out about, and/or visited the following trouble spots: Argentina, Biafra, Bosnia, Cambodia, Israel and the occupied West Bank, Paraguay, South Africa, the Soviet Union, and Soviet Jewry. Wiesel's Nobel Address emphasized his commitment. When human lives are endangered, when human dignity is in jeopardy, national borders and sensitivities become irrelevant. Whenever men or women are persecuted because of their race, religion, or political views, that place must—at that moment—become the center of the universe.[2] Furthermore, Wiesel's universal commitment stemmed from his Jewish identity. "I am a Jew," he observed. "It is through Jewishness that I find universality." His concern was intimately related to his Jewish identity.

In the America of the 1960s and '70s, there was an emphasis on civil rights and human rights. Furthermore, "American Jews . . . organized meetings about the plight of Iron Curtain Jews." The Soviet Union was home to the world's second largest diaspora Jewish population. As the prize-winning

American Jewish historian Professor Hasia Diner writes: "American Jews monitored the fate of the Jews in the Soviet Union and Soviet policies vis-à-vis the practice of Judaism, Jewish culture, and the freedom of Soviet Jews to immigrate to Israel, the execution of a group of Jewish activists raised alarm bells."[3] In 1974 Senator Henry "Scoop" Jackson of Washington State, a place where comparatively few Jews lived, was the co-sponsor of the Jackson-Vanik Amendment (along with Ohio Congressman Charles Vanik). Neither man was Jewish. The Jackson-Vanik Amendment was aimed at pressuring the Soviet Union to allow Jews (refuseniks, as they were known) to emigrate to Israel. The Amendment sanctioned all countries which restricted the right to emigrate. Both legislators had served in the American military. Jackson had been in the Buchenwald concentration camp a few days after its liberation. Human rights became increasingly part of American policy concerns; frequently, financial assistance packages mentioned a human rights agenda for recipient countries.

On the Jewish side, Abraham Joshua Heschel, himself a refugee from Nazism and the scion of a renowned European Hasidic dynasty which was obliterated during the Holocaust, was a distinguished faculty member of the Jewish Theological Seminary, where he taught Social Ethics and Mysticism. Heschel, who also opposed the war in Vietnam, had long spoken out on behalf of Soviet Jewry. Professor Frederick Downing contends that Heschel had a profound influence on Wiesel. The older man's voice functioned as the "outward call toward a deeper humanity," notes Downing.[4] Wiesel recalled that the two men spent hours together often walking up and down Riverside Drive discussing "God, prayers, Polish Hasidism compared to Hungarian Hasidism, Lithuanian Yiddish Folklore, and Polish Yiddish Literature."[5]

Wiesel's important 1966 book *The Jews of Silence* marked him as a messenger for the living. He had traveled to Russia one year earlier, his trip coinciding with the Jewish High Holidays. In his "note to the reader" Wiesel writes, "The pages that follow are the report of a witness. Nothing more and nothing else." But the book's pages are indeed something else. They reveal the fear, silence, and determination to remain Jewish on the part of Russia's then three million Jews. Describing the Jewish situation in Russia, Wiesel notes, "Since others try to prevent them from living either as Jews or as non-Jews, they decide . . . to preserve their Jewishness." "Most," he continues, "come to synagogue on Jewish holidays not to pray, not out of a belief in the God of Israel or in His Torah, but out of a desire to identify with the Jewish people—about whom they know next to nothing."[6]

Despite Wiesel's introductory remarks to the contrary, this volume is in fact an indictment. The last two sentences of the work buttress this contention: "I returned from the Soviet Union disheartened and depressed. But what torments me the most is not the Jews of silence I met in Russia, but the silence of the Jews I live among today."[7] Memory is Wiesel's goad. Jews should not remain silent while their co-religionists—both religious and secular—are under threat. This is, according to Wiesel, what happened during the Shoah. Silence always helps the torturer, never his victim.

Wiesel returned to the Soviet Union the following year. At that time, he was trailed by Soviet agents and nearly arrested. There was a genuine concern among the Israeli agents accompanying him that he would be detained in Moscow. He had brought with him published copies of *The Jews of Silence*. There were some tense moments—he notified the office of Senator Jacob Javitz, his New York Senate Representative, that there might be some difficulties leaving Russia. However, at the time, not wanting to upset Marion, he did not notify her of his concerns. Wiesel was in any case spirited onto a plane, and he flew safely back to America.

Wiesel's efforts on behalf of Soviet Jewry continued for over two decades (1966–1990). In addition to his personal reportage in *The Jews of Silence*, he wrote a novel, *The Testament*, whose hero at first abandons Judaism and then becomes a believer before being shot on Stalin's orders; and a play, *Zalman or the Madness of God*, dealing with the religious situation of Jews in the Soviet Union. Wiesel's personal commitment to the spiritual awakening of Soviet Jews to remain Jewish was underscored by his statement, "If I should be remembered—I would hope it would be as a messenger of the young Jews of the Soviet Union." When he was in Israel he frequently would greet the Russian Jews as their planes landed in a remote part of Ben Gurion Airport. Interestingly, Wiesel's approach toward intervening on behalf of Russia's Jews clashed with that of Rabbi Menachem Mendel Schneerson, the Lubvitcher Rebbe. The Rebbe advocated for "quiet diplomacy" in aiding Soviet Jewry, fearing that a public campaign would further jeopardize their future. He later came to agree with Wiesel's approach, writing the Nobel laureate a personal message.

Wiesel reported in his Nobel Lecture that when he left the ceremonial hall, he and his wife returned to their hotel, where they began calling Russian refuseniks in the Soviet Union. "We wanted them to know that," he continued, "especially on this day we were thinking not only of our joy but also of their plight." Soon the refuseniks began calling back. Wiesel terms the entire afternoon "a dialogue of human solidarity." Addressing the members of the Nobel committee on the following day, he pointed to his Nobel Prize's concrete immediate meaning to the Jews in Russia. "It meant that here in this place we care, we think of them, and we shall never forget."[8]

Wiesel's human rights efforts began with the Jewish people, but did not stop there. His human rights concern extended to a host of others.

A partial listing, as noted, includes Biafra, South Africa, the boat people escaping the new communist regime in Vietnam, Rwanda, and the victims of Pol Pot's Khmer Rouge in Cambodia, which has been termed an "auto-genocide." In addition, he traveled to Nicaragua to speak out on behalf of the Miskito tribe, which was being persecuted by Daniel Ortega's left-wing Sandinista regime. Wiesel focused on the tribe, which had formerly lived in Nicaragua and then been expelled by Ortega, who had arrested some, destroyed the homes of others, and executed still others. Eventually, the tribe was allowed to return to their homes. Wiesel observed that in terms of the designation "illegal," while some people may be tall or short, skinny or fat, no human being is "illegal." He also traveled to Argentina to speak on behalf of the journalist Jacobo Timerman, who had been jailed by the right-wing military dictatorship that had taken over the country.

Another cause for which Wiesel fought was the Ache tribe of Paraguay. He published an epigraph to a book compiled by the International League of Human Rights. Edited by Richard Arens, Wiesel's contribution is titled "Now We Know." The government of President Alfredo Stroessner, a Nazi sympathizer, was implementing a so-called development policy which in reality involved the murder of indigenous tribes that were viewed as an impediment to the nation's interest in mining and cattle raising. Wiesel was horrified by what he discovered, especially since there were familiar signs reminding him of the Holocaust. The males were murdered for pleasure. Young girls were raped and then sold. Children were murdered in front of their parents. It was, attested Wiesel, no accident that these events were occurring in Paraguay. Dr. Joseph Mengele, the "Angel of Death" from Auschwitz-Birkenau, resided in the country as a guest of Stroessner. Wiesel noted that Mengele would be pleased to advise on another "Final Solution." He said that now we know, but indifference seemed to gain the upper hand.[9]

Describing his experiences witnessing apartheid in South Africa, Wiesel wrote: "It is man within you, white man, who feels himself reduced to shame. You lower your eyes so as not to see South Africa." Wiesel continued, "What strikes one about apartheid is its pettiness as well as its cruelty." Speculating about the Jewish future of the country, Wiesel noted that "the whites object to the liberal ideas of the Jews, while the blacks reject them because of their color."[10]

And about Biafra, "Your dead numbered in the hundreds, then the thousands. But tell me friends, where did you bury them? I know where: in the eyes of your children."[11] Once again, the story repeats itself: indifference, impotence, and the innocent are murdered on what Hegel called the slaughter bench of history.

In 1980 on the 18th day of the Jewish month of Shivat, Wiesel was standing on the border between Thailand and Cambodia in the dusty village of Aranyaprathet. He gathered a minyan to say *kaddish* for his father. Behind him he heard a voice choked with sobs. "Who are you saying *kaddish* for?", Wiesel asked. The owner of the choked voice pointed across the border to say "for them" (the Cambodians).[12]

On April 23, 1993, at the dedication of the United States Holocaust Memorial Museum, Wiesel, who had recently returned from a trip to the former Yugoslavia, reproached President Bill Clinton about American passivity in the Balkans. Standing under a blackened sky, in a torrential downpour and a panoply of umbrellas, the Holocaust survivor spoke truth to power. "Mr. President," said Wiesel, "I cannot not tell you something. I cannot sleep. We must stop the bloodshed in that country [Bosnia]. People fight each other and children die. Why? Something, anything must be done."[13] President Clinton, while miffed by this rebuke, acted, but only much later. Wiesel's trip to Bosnia did not go well. Although he was promised that there would be no retaliation against prisoners who spoke with him, this promise was broken. It is estimated that over 8,000 Bosnians were murdered in the war. Two generals, first Ratko Mladic ("the Butcher of Bosnia") and then Radovan Karadžić, were tried at the international war crimes tribunal at the Hague. They were convicted of war crimes and crimes against humanity. Charges included the Srebrencia massacre.

Additionally, Wiesel befriended the Dalai Lama and protested to China about that country's subjugation of Tibet and its expulsion of the Holy Man. Wiesel also supported the Armenians in their stories of Turkish genocidal terror against the Armenian people in the First World War. He also testified against Klaus Barbie, the "Butcher of Lyon," for torturing Jews and members of the resistance before sending them to Auschwitz.

Assessing what he termed the "anatomy of hate," Wiesel turned to the biblical tale of Cain and Abel. Cain slew his brother for no apparent reason, what in Hebrew is termed *sinat henam* (causeless hatred). While the world has advanced technologically by light years since the biblical era, humans have still not solved the problem of murder and violence. Moreover, hate is the twin of fanaticism. Both are opposed to dialogue, which sensitizes us to the needs of our fellow humans. Fanatics have no need for dialogue because they already possess all the answers. This emphasis on American inter-faith dialogue coincided with an increasing sense of its importance in various countries' religious lives, although America took the lead in this area. University and Adult Education courses in interreligious dialogue were growing in popularity. Rabbis and ministers frequently addressed each other's congregations. Many Christians attended Passover Seders. There seemed to be a genuine quest for interreligious understanding.

Looking to the future, however, Wiesel observed that "fanaticism (whether political or religious) is the real danger threatening the twenty-first century. Those who sow it today are provoking tomorrow's catastrophes."[14] It certainly is the case that we are currently living in an era of increasing religious fundamentalism and political extremism. Dialogue, Wiesel observed, always involves three parties: two human beings and God, and enables people to speak and listen to each other. This permits time to reflect and to grow spiritually. Fanatics, however, are those who either act or speak in God's name or, worse, contend that they themselves are divinities. These people, attested Wiesel, turn their God into a killer. The rise of authoritarian governments both in America and Europe is a worrisome sign in our time. In America, one can see how the actions and statements of a reckless and ill-informed president and his many enablers can wreak political havoc. In addition to Donald Trump, one thinks of South American authoritarians such as Venezuela's Nicolas Madura and Brazil's Jair Bolsonaro. European dictators include Hungary's Victor Orban, Poland's Andrzej Duda and Recep Tayyip Erdogan of Turkey. These individuals collectively pose a great threat to the democratic process and to Wiesel's understanding of dialogue.

WIESEL AND ISRAEL

Wiesel was an *Ohav Yisroel* (lover of Israel) above all else, and was that county's passionate defender as it came under unremitting criticism from both the left and the right.

The assaults, usually under a variety of disguises such as anti-Zionism, provided a perfect cover for antisemitism. It's not the Jewish people we dislike, claimed the anti-Zionists, it is rather the actions of the State of Israel. Official institutions such as the United Nations regularly condemn the Jewish State while remaining silent in the face of actions by member nations that are egregious violators of human rights. Quasi-political movements such as BDS (Boycott, Divest, and Sanction) also regularly condemn Israel. It is noteworthy to recall that the founder of this movement, Omar Barghouti, contends that Israel alone of all the nations has no right to exist. Palestinians taking sides with Israel don't represent BDS and the rest of Palestinians, and that international artists who perform in Israel are complicit exclaims Barghouti. (https://www.youtube.com/watch?v=syc WQJXNniy). Professor Curtis Maroz The American Studies Association president at that time said that in working for social change you have to start somewhere. Email from Professor Dan Berger (1/24/2021) The resolution was widely criticized by Israel and over 200 universities (Wikipedia)., https://en.wikipedia.org/wiki/American_Studies_Association%27s_boycott_ of_Israel#:~:text=In%20December%202013%2C%20members%20of, rights%20violations%20against%20the%20Palestinians.

This is not to contend that Israel is above criticism. Far from it. Israel is a modern nation state that like other modern nations makes political mistakes. However, one needs to separate legitimate political opposition from antisemitism. Natan Sharansky, a former refusenik who has been living in Israel since his release from Russian confinement, has suggested an important barometer for, on the one hand, gauging legitimate criticism of the State of Israel, and, on the other hand, antisemitism. Sharansky notes that when any of the following three D's are involved, one has moved beyond politics and into Jew hatred: Delegitimation (Israel has no right to exist), Demonization (Israel is the cause of the world's problems), and Double standard (Israel is to be judged according to standards that apply to no other country). The American State Department has endorsed the Sharansky definition.

Wiesel was widely criticized by the left, which accused him of ignoring the plight of the Palestinians. This view was especially pronounced among adherents of the so-called liberation theology movement, as in Mark Chmiel's 2001 book *Elie Wiesel and the Politics of Moral Leadership*.[15] He accuses Wiesel of remaining silent about the Palestinians and their suffering under Israeli rule. In the first place, Wiesel did not remain silent. He said in his Nobel Address, "Of course since I am a Jew profoundly rooted in my people's memory and tradition, my first response is to Jewish fears, Jewish needs, Jewish crises. It would be unnatural not to make Jewish priorities my own."[16] "But," he continued, "others are important to me." He said apartheid was as abhorrent as antisemitism. He also mentioned the disgraceful isolation in the Soviet Union of the non-Jewish dissident Andrei Sakharov and the imprisonment and exile of the Jewish activists Josef Begun and Ida Nudel. He continued by noting "the denial of Solidarity and its leader Lech Walesa's right to dissent. And Nelson Mandela's interminable imprisonment."[17]

Specifically concerning the Palestinians, Wiesel sympathized with their situation but deplored their use of violence and murder. Both in public lectures and in print he emphasized this point. In his 1970 "Letter to a Young Palestinian Arab," he wrote, "The arguments on both sides are valid." Irritated by Palestinian threats, he was "overwhelmed by your suffering."[18] What divides Jews and Palestinians is their attitude toward suffering. "For you," wrote Wiesel, "it seems to justify everything; not for me."[19] "While feeling responsible for what happened to you, I do not [feel responsible] for what you choose to do as a result of what happened to you."[20] Everything depends on "humanizing suffering."[21] Later, in a conversation with Philippe de Saint-Cheron, Wiesel emphatically stated that "unlike leftists and revolutionaries, I do not consider the Palestinians today's 'Jews.' . . . They are not threatened with extermination as we, the Jews, were during the war."[22] Moreover, he referred to the Palestinians in his Oslo (Nobel) speech, saying, "I am sensitive to their suffering, but I deplore their methods when they lead to violence."[23] Wiesel continued, "The Jewish people and the Palestinian people have lost too many children and have shed too much blood since 1948: it is time to stop."[24] As a Jew, "it is only natural that [my] loyalty and love go first to Israel. Just as it is natural for a Palestinian's love and loyalty to go first to his people."[25]

The issue of Israel is complex. As a Holocaust survivor, Wiesel was well aware that no country wanted the Jews during World War II. If the Jewish State had existed at that time, the cattle cars headed for Auschwitz would have been less full and Jews would not have been abandoned. Yet, when he was twice offered the presidency of the Jewish State, first by Prime Minister Ehud Olmert in 2006 and then eight years later by Prime Minister Benjamin Netanyahu, he declined. His son, Elisha, contends that his father was concerned about the amount of time he would have to write his books if he were to have accepted the offers.

Wiesel viewed himself as a writer and a teacher. He had neither the time nor the inclination to assume an office which could easily be submerged in politics. However, Wiesel always advocated for the position that Jews not living in Israel should refrain from criticizing the Jewish State in public. When Israel faced a crisis, Wiesel always flew to the Jewish State. He was there for the Six Day War. His novel *A Beggar in Jerusalem* merges the Holocaust past with Israel's victory in that war. He writes that the reason Israel won is because it could deploy six million more soldiers.

As an activist, Wiesel was heavily involved with both Yad Vashem, Israel's national Holocaust memorial center and research museum, and with the United States Holocaust Memorial Museum. He helped in coordinating activities and exhibits. The Swedish prime minister invited him to be the honorary chair of the Stockholm Conference on Conscience and Humanity, which eventuated in the creation of the International Holocaust Remembrance Alliance. Professor Steven T. Katz, Wiesel's long-time Boston University colleague, mentions two other episodes. Despite his unwavering support of Israel, he distanced himself from Prime Minister Benjamin Netanyahu after the politician violated a commitment he had made to Wiesel concerning a political appointment which Wiesel was not that keen about in the first place Nevertheless, he sat in the congressional visitors' gallery when Netanyahu spoke on an unofficial visit to America. And, despite supporting President Obama, Wiesel wrote an open letter in 2010 urging the president not to pressure Israel over the issue of the settlements and Jerusalem. "For me, the Jew that I am, Jerusalem is above politics." It should also be noted that Wiesel continued to criticize Iran, even though he believed he could become a target of Iranian assassins.[26]

Concerning fanaticism—religious or political—Wiesel observed that it is the real danger threatening the twenty-first century. The religious fanatic, he wrote, is "convinced that he is the sole possessor of the meaning of life, [therefore] he gags or kills the other in order not to be challenged . . . and finally, the religious fanatic sees God not as his judge and king, but as his prisoner."[27] Combating fanaticism (which is the major component of hate, and vice versa) "means denouncing the humiliation of the Other. It means celebrating the freedom of the Other, the freedom of all Others."[28] "To hate," continued Wiesel, "is to refuse to accept another person as a human being, to diminish him."[29] Furthermore, Wiesel distinguished types of hatred and their consequences.

> Religious hatred makes the face of God invisible. Political hatred wipes out people's liberties. In the field of science, hatred inevitably puts itself at death's service. In literature it distorts truth, perverts the meaning of the story and hides beauty itself under a thick layer of blood and grime.[30]

As a Nobel Peace laureate, Wiesel kept a steadfast eye on his goal of moving the world in the direction of peace and dialogue. Moreover, this was an intergenerational task. From involving young people in the international conferences he co-sponsored with the king of Jordan, to the Wiesel Foundation's essay contest, Wiesel's efforts were focused on the task of helping achieve both a *tikkun ha-olam* and a *tikkun atzmi*—a repair of the world and a repair of the self. These repairs are necessary steps on the road to world peace and must continue especially in the face of historical adversity.

Notes

1. Elie Wiesel, *From the Kingdom of Memory: Reminiscences.* New York: Summit Books, 1990, page 248. Hereafter this work will be cited as *FKM.*
2. Ibid., page 233.
3. Hasia R. Dinvr, *We Remember With Reverence and Love: American Jews and the Myth of Silence After the Holocaust 1945–1962.* New York: New York University Press, 2009, page 282.
4. Frederick Downing, *Elie Wiesel: A Religious Biography.* Macon, GA: Mercer University Press, 2008, page 174.
5. Elie Wiesel, *All Rivers Run to the Sea: Memoirs.* Translated by Marion Wiesel. New York: Alfred A. Knopf, 1995, page 353.
6. Elie Wiesel, *The Jews of Silence.* Translated by Neal Kozodoy. New York: Holt Rinehart & Winston Inc., 1966, page 114.
7. Ibid., page 127.
8. *FKM*, page 247.
9. Wiesel's Epilogue reads in part: "This tribe is being exterminated so that nothing will remain not even a cry or a tear. Efficient technique tested elsewhere is used here: the individual is dragged away from his tribe, and of his memory too. He is diminished. He is forced to look at himself through the eyes of his enemy in order to become his own enemy, and thus wish

his own death." Irving Abrahamson (editor), *Against Silence: The Voice and Vision of Elie Wiesel*. New York City: Holocaust Library, 1985, volume II, pages 371–372.

10. Elie Wiesel. *A Jew Today* Translated by Marion Wiesel. New York Vintage Books.page 64 1979.

11. Elie Wiesel. *A Jew Today* Translated by Marion Wiesel. New York Vintage Books.page 36 1979.

12. Elie Wiesel, *And the Sea Is Never Full*. Translated by Marion Wiesel. New York: Alfred A. Knopf, 1999, page 91.

13. Elie Wiesel at the dedication of the United States Holocaust Memorial Museum, Washington, DC, April 2, 1993.

14. Ibid.

15. Mark Chmiel, *Elie Wiesel and the Politics of Moral Leadership*. Philadelphia: Temple University Press, 2001.

16. *FKM*, page 233.

17. Ibid.

18. Elie Wiesel, *A Jew Today*. Translated by Marion Wiesel. New York: Vintage Books, 1979, page 123. Hereafter this work will be cited as *AJT*.

19. Ibid., page 126.

20. Ibid., page 127.

21. Ibid.

22. Elie Wiesel and Philippe Michael de Saint-Cheron, Editors, *Evil and Exile*. Translated by Jon Rothschild. Notre Dame: University of Notre Dame Press, 1990, page 21.

23. Ibid., page 21.

24. Ibid., pages 21–22.

25. Ibid.

26. Steven T. Katz, "Elie Wiesel: The Man and His Legacy," *Yad Vashem Studies*, December 2016, pages 19–20.

27. *AJT*, page 371.

28. Ibid., page 372.

29. Ibid., page 376.

30. Ibid., pages 366–367.

CHAPTER 6

WIESEL'S SEARCH FOR WORLD PEACE

World peace is as elusive as it is desirable. It is chimerical in nature, reminding us of the tale of Sisyphus and his fabled boulder. According to the legend, Sisyphus was tasked with endlessly rolling a boulder up a mountain peak. As soon as the summit was approached, the boulder rolled back down again. There is neither surrender nor absolute victory in this process. There is, instead, a resolute steadfastness of purpose. Nonetheless, Albert Camus imagined Sisyphus happy. I asked Elie Wiesel if he believed Sisyphus was happy. He responded in characteristic Wieselian fashion: "Yes and no."[1] Wiesel viewed Sisyphus as oscillating. Perhaps he is one thing when on top of the mountain and another when he is below. "Maybe," speculated Wiesel, "he has done it so often that he forgets that he will go up." Unlike Sisyphus, however, Wiesel never forgot his mission to fight for human rights and world peace, even though there were times when he thought that the world had learned nothing from the Holocaust and the far too many genocides that followed. But Wiesel fully embraced his mission as a witness. In this sense he represents both the optimism of *Souls on Fire* and the fragments of despair found in the pages of *Four Hasidic Masters and Their Struggle Against Melancholy*.

When he and Marion established The Elie Wiesel Foundation for Humanity shortly after he won the 1986 Nobel Prize, they had a grand vision: combating hatred and working to defeat fanaticism. The Foundation's mission certainly faced a steep ascent in overcoming world-wide hatred. The mission statement, rooted in memory of the Holocaust, is to "combat indifference, intolerance and injustice through international dialogue and youth-focused programs that promote acceptance, understanding and equality."[2] Nonetheless, it approached its mission in a manner that permitted the achievement of certain goals in a world that had witnessed the resurgence of antisemitism, racism, terrorism, and the disparagement of the Other. As the problems were multi-faceted, so too was the Foundation's response. The response began, but did not end, with Wiesel's commitment to teaching. First and foremost was his resolve to involve his students in the task of achieving *tikkun ha-olam* (repair of the world). This involved a variety of social justice projects wherever injustice may occur, protesting against war, feeding and sheltering the homeless, and joining the Peace Corps.

His concern for his students buoyed them in uncertain times. No matter where in the world he happened to be, Wiesel always called in to his classes at Boston University. His commitment, however, extended beyond his Boston University students. My seminar students at Florida Atlantic University were greatly enriched when Wiesel agreed to speak with them via conference call. We would speak about whichever of his novels we happened to be reading at the time. Among the topics we discussed were Hasidism, the issue of God's role in the Holocaust, and the human condition after Auschwitz. My students were transformed by these sessions. Wiesel himself viewed teaching as "a sharing of determination, that mine will become a part of your determination, so that you will continue doing good things after I am gone."[3] Consequently, teaching is a mission and forms part of the effort of pushing the boulder up the mountain peak.

The Foundation soon became international in scope, holding four conferences in Petra, Jordan, under the joint sponsorship of The King Abdullah II Fund for Development and The Elie Wiesel Foundation for Humanity. The issue of the West Bank and the Palestinians, among other topics, was raised at Petra IV under the general heading "Growth and Economic Development in the Middle East: The Way Forward." The conference was held in 2008, but its full proceedings have not yet appeared. The Palestinian President, Mohammed Abbas, was present. These conferences attracted Nobel laureates from many fields and from many countries in order to deal with issues that threaten peace. Addressing the delegates at the first Petra conference of Nobel laureates (May 2005), Wiesel had no illusions. "We are on a runaway train," he attested, "hurtling toward the abyss. Do we have the determination to stop it? It will not be easy—but we must lest our past become our children's future."[4] Delegates at the second Petra conference, "A World in Danger" (June 2006), heard King Abdullah lament the fact that "in today's world, where unprecedented prosperity exists alongside widespread deprivation; . . . modern humanity has not yet grasped its global responsibilities."[5]

The third Petra conference (May 2007) continued the theme of a world in danger. Among the participants were the Dalai Lama and youth from the Middle East. Among the topics discussed were education, science, health, the economy, and the environment. Petra IV (June 2008) grappled with brainstorming around issues such as "The Hunger Crisis," "Investing in Youth Using Innovative Educational Tools," "Advances in Medicine," "Arts and Culture," "Energy," and "Growth and Economic Development in the Middle East." These topics became "teaching moments," and Wiesel fervently believed that teaching is a form of activism. Applying themselves to solving these problems made the issue seem just a little bit more manageable. Participants also got a chance to mingle with and be inspired by leaders such as Vaclav Havel and Nelson Mandela, former political prisoners who had become world leaders.

To further advance its peace building agenda, the Foundation established the Beit Tzipora Centers for Study and Enrichment. Two centers in Israel, one in Ashkelon and the second in Kiryat Malachi, focus on educating the Ethiopian Jewish community. In the mid-1990s over 14,000 Ethiopian Jews were rescued from persecution in Africa and brought to Israel in Operation Solomon (May 24–25, 1991). The Beit Tzipora Centers, named after Wiesel's little sister murdered in the Shoah, assist these Jewish-Ethopian youngsters to adjust to, and succeed in, Israeli life. Currently the schools enroll over 1,000 pupils. Both Elie and Marion Wiesel were actively engaged with these schools, visiting often to encourage the students.

In America, the Wiesel Foundation annually sponsors the Elie Wiesel Ethics Essay Contest, which is open to American university juniors and seniors. In the more than 30 years since its inception, the Foundation has received thousands of essays, including some written by incarcerated prisoners. Two essays remain with me. One, written by a lifer, dealt with the issue of justice and the prisoner's outreach to his fellow inmates. The second was written by a young Brown University student who argued against reducing people to their essentialism. Two books devoted to the essay contest have appeared recently: *Elie Wiesel: Teacher, Mentor and Friend* (Alan L. Berger, editor, Cascade Books, 2018), and *Ethical Compass*. Introduction by Elie Wiesel and preface by Thomas Friedman.

The essay contest continues to flourish, even after Wiesel's passing. It recently celebrated its 31st year. Students are asked to reflect on a societal problem in ethics. An eight-person Reader's Committee comprised of both Christians and Jews, females and males, chooses the best essays, which are then sent to the judges for the final round. There is a first, second, and third prize, along with two Honorable Mentions. The winners are invited to New York City for a seminar. Each student comments on her/his fellow students' essays. Discussions are typically robust and insightful. The seminar is led by a member of the Reader's Committee. Participants then meet with Mr. Dov Seidman, former Chairperson of the Legal Research Network (LRN, an ethics and compliance management firm); partner to The Elie Wiesel Foundation for Humanity). Prior to his passing, Wiesel also met and dined with the student winners their families, other invited guests, and members of the readers committee. Each of the students then speaks briefly about their project and what the contest has meant to their lives. Student projects are as varied as the students themselves. Examples include genocide prevention, societal indifference, the Othering of the Other, and difficult decisions, like when to turn off the ventilator.

I vividly recall leading my first seminar. I told Wiesel afterward that the experience had renewed my hope for the future. These young people are the ones who will be dealing with complicated issues and it is good that they are getting a head start. The students share a commitment to making a difference in the world and want to make a positive impact on society. Wiesel enthusiastically responded, "Yes, Alan, this is why Marion and I established the contest. We want to provide an opportunity for students to help make a better world." The contest celebrated its 30th anniversary in 2019 at New York City's Jewish Museum. There is much evidence to support the claim that the students keep in touch with one another, thus forming a kind of mini think-tank.

The Foundation also sponsors a series of international conferences, in addition to the Petra meetings. The goal of these conferences is to help "create a world in which atrocities such as the Holocaust, and genocide in Rwanda and Darfur and ethnic cleansing" in Bosnia are never forgotten, but also never repeated. To date, the Foundation has sponsored eight such international conferences: Paris (1988), whose theme was "Facing the 21st Century: Threats and Promises"; Haifa, Israel (1990), "Education Against Hate: An Imperative for Our Time"; Oslo (1990), "The Oslo Conference: The Anatomy of Hate: Resolving Conflict Through Dialogue and Democracy"; Moscow (1991), "The Moscow Conference: The Anatomy of Hate"; New York (1992), "The New York Conference: The Anatomy of Hate, Saving Our Children"; Venice (1995), "Conference of Tomorrow's Leaders"; Tokyo (1995), "The Future of Hope Conference"; and Boston (2000), "Conference of Tomorrow's Leaders: From Indifference to Action." These conferences bring together Nobel laureates, other distinguished thinkers, and youth in order to seek possible ways forward in a world that is both full of promise and ambushed by pitfalls.

Wiesel's work begs the question of the relationship between the universal and the particular. He wrote,

> For a Jew, the only way to be human is to be Jewish. A Jew who believes he must shake off his past and his identity simply to go farther and higher is a fool. He cannot go farther. He can attain universality only from within his Jewishness.[6]

As a "messenger of peace," Wiesel always embraced his identity, not as a weapon of separation, or a "problem" for others, but as a stimulation for the universality of his claims. He approvingly endorsed the contention of his friend, fellow survivor, and international attorney Samuel Pisar, who observed in his 1979 award-winning Holocaust memoir *Of Blood and Hope*, that it always starts with the Jews but never ends with them. For Wiesel, "whatever happened to the Jewish people is only the beginning" (Literature and Belief 26.1, 2005 p.2). Israel has become the "Jew among the nations," alone subjected to baseless antisemitic claims, on the part of the Russians and many extremists in the Arab world, of being the "new Nazis," bent on the obliteration of the Arab peoples. As long as false stereotypes such as these exist, they will clearly require massive educational projects to correct.

Wiesel did not accept the commonly made distinctions between Jew and man; they are not opposites and do not cancel each other out. To be a Jew today, therefore, means to testify, to bear witness to what is and to what is no longer. One can testify with joy, though tainted with sadness, by aiding Israel, or with anger—restrained, harnessed anger free of sterile bitterness— by raking over the ashes of the Holocaust. For the contemporary Jewish writer, there can be no theme more human, no project more universal.[7]

Wiesel's way was the way of dialogue. Extremists had nothing to add to the discussion, because they already knew all the answers. All one could do in the face of such arrogance was to shut up and listen. The non-dialog-ical model has resulted in many wars, border incursions, and other signs that sabotage peace and efforts at mutual understanding. The American presidential election of 2016 ushered in a chilling atmosphere concerning the possibility of dialogue that continued with the 2020 election.The Biden presidency offers hope for the restoration of civility and the possibility of reason over irrationality. Our society would do well to remember that dia-logue is no sign of weakness. Rather, it is a process by which difficult truths can be confronted and causeless hatred overcome. Lack of a common lan-guage has in the past doomed mankind (Tower of Babel), and it may well do the same in the future.

Wiesel drew hope from his family, which includes his wife Marion, his son, Elisha, and daughter-in-law Lynn Bartner-Wiesel. His grandson Eli-jah (born 2005), and granddaughter Shira (born 2008) were very special to him. Elisha retired after 25 years at Goldman Sachs, where he was the Chief Information Officer. Currently he is engaged in philanthropic efforts and chairs the Tel-Aviv based Israeli vender management outfit "The Floor" He also is dealing with his father's papers and speaks about the contemporary impact of Elie Wiesel. Lynn Bartner-Wiesel is the Executive Officer of the America-Israel Cultural Foundation.

Open Heart his last published book, describes both his physical condition (in 2011 he had a quintuple by pass operation; his heart was literally opened) and is a metaphor for how Elie Wiesel faced the world. He was a man of faith, and prayer, who sought to heal the wounds humanity inflected upon itself and the Other.

I began thinking about this book when Elie was still alive. Now, five years after his passing, it was time to reflect on his life. It is no easy task to know when to conclude a study of Elie Wiesel. He himself wrote that despite his nearly sixty books, he felt he was just beginning. Peace is a jealous mistress who requires full time attention. It is with this in mind that we close, at least for now, our discussion of Elie Wiesel, Man of Peace. Elie poignantly wrote in *Open Heart* "I desperately want to keep the promise to my son, Elisha to be present at Elijah's Bar Mitzvah and perhaps even at Shira's Bat Mitzvah' (page 79). Sadly, for both his family and humanity, Elie was unable to keep his promise.

An appropriate tale comes to mind here.

"poor stranger. You shout, you expend yourself body and soul,
Don't you see that it is hopeless" "Yes, I see." Answered the
Just man.
"Then why do you go on"
"I'll tell you why. In the beginning, I thought that I
Could change man. Today, I know I cannot
If I still shout today, if I still scream, it is to
Prevent man from ultimately changing me." [8]

But despair is never the way Wiesel ended his message. *Open Heart*, leaves his readers with a type of theological and cultural road map with which to traverse life's anti-genocidal path. There is of course the perennial question first posed in *Night*: what about God in all of this? There is also guidance for the perplexed:

> I still believe in man in spite of man. I believe in language even though it is wounded . . . and I continue to cling to words because it is up to us to transform them into instruments of comprehension rather than contempt. It is up to us to choose whether we wish to use them to curse or heal, to wound or to console.[9]

Notes

1. Alan L. Berger, "Interview With Elie Wiesel," *Literature and Belief*, 26, no. 1, 2006, page 21.
2. "Mission Statement," *The Elie Wiesel Foundation for Humanity*, page 2.
3. Ariel Burger, *Witness: Lessons From Elie Wiesel's Classroom*. Boston: Houghton Mifflin Harcourt, 2018, page 147.
4. Elie Wiesel, First Petra Conference of Nobel Laureates, May 2005.
5. Second Petra Conference, "A World in Danger," June 2006.

6. Elie Wiesel, *One Generation After*. Translated by Lily Edelman and Elie Wiesel. New York: Shocken Books, 1985, page 174.
7. Ibid.
8. Wiesel, *One Generation After* page 174.
9. Elie Wiesel, *Open Heart*. Translated by Marion Wiesel. New York: Alfred A. Knopf, 2012, page 73.

DOCUMENTS

NIGHT

Key concepts from Wiesel's canonical memoir revealing the extent of the shattering of his pre-Holocaust religious world view.

———————

Never shall I forget that night, the first night in camp, that
Turned my life into one long night seven times sealed.
Never shall I forget that smoke.
Never shall I forget the small faces of the children whose bod-
Ies I saw transformed into smoke under a silent sky.
Never shall I forget those flames that consumed my faith for-
Ever.
Never shall I forget the nocturnal silence that deprived me for
All eternity of the desire to live.
Never shall I forget those moments that murdered my God
And my soul and turned my dreams to ashes.
Never shall I forget those things, even were I condemned to
Live as long as God Himself.
Never.

The night had passed completely. The morning star shone in
The sky. I too had become a different person. The student of
Talmud, the child I was, had been consumed by the flames. All
That was left was a shape that resembled me. My soul had been
Invaded—and devoured—by a black flame.

Behind me, I heard the same man asking:
"For God's sake, where is God?"

And from within me, I heard a voice answer:
"Where He is? This is where—hanging here from this gal-
Lows . . ."
That night, the soup tasted of corpses.

The final scene in the English translation portrays Wiesel looking at himself in a mirror for the first time since he'd been deported.

> From the depths of the mirror, a corpse was contemplating Me.
> The look in his eyes as he gazed at me has never left me.

SOURCE

Elie Wiesel. *Night*, Translated by Marion Wiesel. New York: Hill and Wang, 2006, pages 34, 37, 65, 115.

· DOCUMENT **2**

TO OUR CHILDREN

Excerpt from keynote address given at plenary session of the first International Conference of Children of Holocaust Survivors, New York, May 28, 1984.

When other people want to learn about the Holocaust, they look for generalities. They want to learn how it happened, how much, the magnitude, the scope, figures, facts. What you want is something very specific. You want to study that event in its most human dimension. For you the war has a face—the face of your father, the face of your mother . . .

What we ask of you, therefore, is not easy. We ask you not to forget what we desperately wanted to remember. We ask you to do what we have tried to do—and more: to keep our tale alive—and sacred. Do not allow it to be trivialized . . .

Your task is to be the guardians of that tale. . .

Remember, my young friends, the responsibility of your parents was solely towards the dead: yours will be towards us. . .

We look at one another with pride and gratitude and we think that whatever happened to Abraham and Isaac has happened to us too. The Akedah, after all, was not consummated. The testimony of our life and death will not vanish. Our memories will not die with us.

Do you know what we see in you, in all of you? We see in you our heirs, our allies, our younger brothers and sisters. But in a strange way to all of us all of you are our children.

SOURCE

Irving Abrahamson (editor), *Against Silence: The Voice and Vision of Elie Wiesel.* New York: Holocaust Library, 1985, pages 319–324.

HOW DO YOU VIEW THE RISE
OF RELIGION?

I feel religion must be a humanizing experience. If religion becomes a tool in the hands of a fanatic, then it is bad religion and that fanatic betrays God, just as he or she betrays people. And unfortunately, fanaticism and religion have gone hand in hand for too long. I'm afraid of that. Once you believe that whatever you do you do in the name of a higher power, that you do it for the sake of God, it's dangerous. And I would like to believe that as a Jew, I am what I am. And I respect those who are not Jewish. As somebody who does come from a religious background, I have tried to define myself from within that tradition, but I respect anyone who does not belong to that tradition, as long as that spirit of tolerance is shared. I don't want to be faced with intolerance, for that I have to answer a different way.

SOURCE

Elie Wiesel and Richard D. Heffner, *Conversations With Elie Wiesel.* Edited by Thomas J. Vinciguerra. New York: Schocken Books, 2003, page 69.

REFUSING TO GIVE IN TO DESPAIR AND HATRED

Excerpt from Wiesel's response to a student in his Boston University class, fall semester 2006.

After the war I did come close to despair. I felt hatred for those who were silent, but I rejected that. Hatred is a kind of cancer, and, unlike anger, it serves no purpose. And I was not willing to give up my soul to hatred and despair. It was a choice. And my tradition is filled with hope. In spite of three thousand years of suffering and difficulty, it is a celebration. I was fortunate to be born into this tradition of celebration, and that gave me the strength to reject hatred, to reject despair.

Rather than hate, rather than despair, I chose the path of protest, of rebellion, of refusal to accept human suffering. I have tried to live my life against silence. When victims have no voice, I try to lend them mine. When they feel alone, I try to show them they are not by going to them and by writing and speaking about their suffering. This is not enough, but it is something. Had we, in 1944 in my little town, felt that we were not alone, it would have made a difference. But precisely because we felt alone, no one else ever should.

SOURCE

Ariel Burger, *Witness: Lessons From Elie Wiesel's Classroom*. New York: Houghton Mifflin Harcourt Publishing Company, 2018, pages 125–126.

The Difference Between the Crusades and Auschwitz

Excerpt from interview, 2006.

———

I felt for a long time and I still do that Christianity, because of what has been done to the Jews, lost many of its values in Auschwitz. In a way it was a defeat of Christianity, because it happened in the heart of Europe which was a Christian continent. Both Catholics and Protestants were baptized. Hitler himself was baptized. But to compare it to the Crusades, no. The Crusades were in a way actually worse because they did whatever they did in the name of Christ. The crusaders carried a crucifix. They went and killed and killed in the name of Christ. In Germany they did "not" kill in the name of Christ. They did it for Germany, for German power, for German glory, for German interests. What they said was for the sake of Germany and not for Jesus. To make things easier for the Catholics? No I do not think so. They have enough to atone for and Christians have enough to reflect on. And by the way, the fact that the Christians were killers, that hurts the good young Germans. They do not sleep at night. The killers were Christians. But only the killers are guilty.

Source

Alan L. Berger. "Interview of Elie Wiesel," *Literature and Belief*, 26, 2006, page 216.

BUCHENWALD CONCENTRATION CAMP

Buchenwald Concentration Camp on April 16, 1945. Elie Wiesel is in the second row from bottom, seventh face from the left.

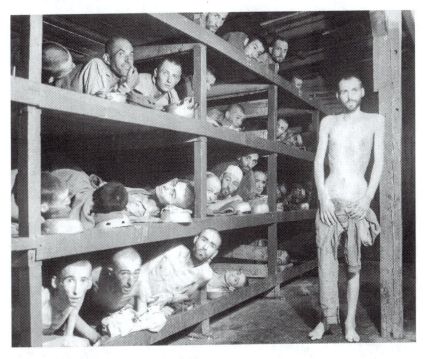

Source: Alpha Historica/Alamy Stock Photo

WIESEL RECEIVES THE GERMAN FEDERAL CROSS OF MERIT

German Foreign Minister Frank-Walter Steinmeier presents Wiesel with the German Federal Cross of Merit. Marion Wiesel also pictured. New York City, September 23, 2014.

Source: dpa picture alliance/Alamy Stock Photo

WIESEL RECEIVES THE NOBEL PEACE PRIZE

Elie Wiesel receives the Nobel Peace Prize, son Elisha also pictured, as is Egil Aarvick.

Source: Courtesy of The Elie Wiesel Foundation for Humanity

ELIE WIESEL WITH PRESIDENT RONALD REAGAN

ACCEPTING THE UNITED STATES CONGRESSIONAL MEDAL
FROM PRESIDENT RONALD REAGAN, APRIL 19, 1985

Source: Courtesy of The Elie Wiesel Foundation for Humanity

DOCUMENT **10**

ELIE WIESEL WITH PRESIDENT BARACK OBAMA

Source: White House Photo/Alamy Stock Photo

BIBLIOGRAPHY

BOOKS

Aarons, Victoria and Phyllis Lassner (co-editors). *The Palgrave Handbook of Holocaust Literature and Culture*. Cham, Switzerland: Springer, 2020.

Abrahamson, Irving (editor). *Against Silence: The Voice and Vision of Elie Wiesel*. New York: Holocaust Library, 1985, three volumes.

Bar-On, Dan. *Legacy of Silence*. Cambridge, MA: Harvard University Press, 1989.

Berenbaum, Michael. *Elie Wiesel: God, the Holocaust, and the Children of Israel*. West Orange: Behrman House, Inc., 1994.

Berger, Alan L. (editor). *Judaism in the Modern World*. New York: New York University Press, 1994.

———. *Children of Job: American Second-Generation Witnesses to the Holocaust*. Albany: SUNY Press, 1997.

——— (editor). *Elie Wiesel: Teacher, Mentor, and Friend*. Eugene, OR: Cascade Books, 2018.

Berger, Alan L. and Victoria Aarons. *Third Generation Holocaust Representation: Trauma, History and Memory*. Evanston, IL: Northwestern University Press, 2017.

Berger, Alan L., Harry Cargas and Susan E. Nowak (editors). *The Continuing Agony: From the Carmelite Convent to the Crosses at Auschwitz*. Academic Studies in the History of Judaism. Binghamton, NY: Global Publications, Binghamton University, 2002.

Berger, Peter. *The Sacred Canopy: Elements of a Sociological Theory of Religion*. New York: Anchor Books, 1969.

Blumenson, Martin. *The Patton Papers 1940–1945*. Boston: Da Capo Press, 2009.

Breitman, Richard and Allan J. Lichtman. *FDR and the Jews*. Cambridge, MA: Harvard University Press, 2013.

Browning, Christopher. *Ordinary Men: Reserve Police Battalion 101 and the Final Solution*. New York: HarperCollins, 2017.

Burger, Ariel. *Witness: Lessons From Elie Wiesel's Classroom*. Boston: Houghton Mifflin Harcourt, 2018.

Cargas, Harry James (editor). *Harry James Cargas in Conversation With Elie Wiesel*. Mahwah, NJ: Paulist Press, 1976.

———. *Conversations With Elie Wiesel*. South Bend, IN: Justice Books, 1992.

Chmiel, Mark. *Elie Wiesel and the Politics of Moral Leadership*. Philadelphia: Temple University Press, 2001.

Dinur, Hasia R. *We Remember With Reverence and Love: American Jews and the Myth of Silence After the Holocaust 1945–1962*. New York: New York University Press, 2009.

Downing, Frederick. *Elie Wiesel: A Religious Biography*. Macon, GA: Mercer University Press, 2008.

Fine, Ellen. *Legacy of Night*. Albany: SUNY Press, 1982.

Franciosi, Robert (editor). *Elie Wiesel: Conversations*. Jackson: University Press of Mississippi, 2002.

Friedman, Maurice. *Abraham Joshua Heschel and Elie Wiesel: You Are My Witnesses*. New York: Farrar, Straus, Giroux, 1987.

Ginzberg, Louis. *The Legends of the Jews*. Translated by Henrietta Szold. Baltimore, MD: The John Hopkins University Press, 1998.

Helmreich, William. *Against All Odds: Holocaust Survivors and the Successful Lives They Made in America*. New Brunswick, NJ: Transaction Publishers, 1996.

Katz, Steven and Alan Rosen (editors). *Elie Wiesel: Jewish, Literary, and Moral Perspectives*. Bloomington: Indiana University Press, 2013.

Lambert, Carol J. *The Judges*. New York: Alfred A. Knopf, 1999.

Laytner, Anson. *Arguing With God: A Jewish Tradition*. Northvale, NJ: Jason Aronson Inc., 1990.

Lipstadt, Deborah E. *Holocaust: An American Understanding*. New Brunswick, NJ: Rutgers University Press, 2016.

Littell, Marcia Sach, Richard Libowitz and Evelyn Bodek-Rosen (editors). "Some Words for Children of Survivors: A Message to the Second Generation," in *The Holocaust Forty Years After*. Lewiston, NY: The Edwin Melon Press, 1989.

McAfee Brown, Robert. *Elie Wiesel: Messenger to All Humanity*. Notre Dame, IN: University of Notre Dame Press, 1989.

Medoff, Rafael. *The Jews Should Keep Quiet: Franklin D. Roosevelt, Rabbi Stephen S. Wise, and the Holocaust*. Lincoln: The University of Nebraska Press and Philadelphia: The Jewish Publication Society, 2019.

Monda, Antonio (editor). *Do You Believe?* Translated by Ann Goldstein. New York: Vintage Books, 2007.

Pressman, Gabe (editor). *A Journey of Faith*. New York: Primus, 1990.

Rosen, Alan (editor). *Celebrating Elie Wiesel: Stories, Essays, Reflections*. Notre Dame, IN: University of Notre Dame Press, 1998.

Roth, John K. *A Consuming Fire: Encounters With Elie Wiesel and the Holocaust*. Atlanta, GA: John Knox Press, 1979.

———. *Sources of Holocaust Insight: Learning and Teaching About the Genocide*. Eugene, OR: Cascade Books, 2020.

Rubenstein, Richard L. "Some Perspectives on Religious Faith After Auschwitz," in *The German Church Struggle and the Holocaust*. Edited by Franklin H. Littell and Hubert G. Locke. Detroit, MI: Wayne State University Press, 1974.

———. *After Auschwitz: History, Theology and Contemporary Judaism*. Second Edition. Baltimore, MD: The Johns Hopkins University Press, 1992.

Sanua-Dalin, Miriam. *Let Us Prove Strong*. Hanover, NH: University Press of New England, 2007.

Sarna, Jonathan. *American Judaism: A History*. New Haven, CT: Yale University Press, 2004.

Wiesel, Elie. *Souls on Fire: Portraits and Legends of Hasidic Masters*. Translated by Marion Wiesel. New York: Random House, 1972.

———. *The Oath*. New York: Avon Books, 1973.

———. *Four Hasidic Masters*. South Bend, IN: Notre Dame University Press, 1978.

———. *A Jew Today*. Translated by Marion Wiesel. New York: Vintage Books, 1979.

———. *Legends of Our Time*. New York: Schocken Books, 1982.

———. *One Generation After*. Translated by Lily Edelman and Elie Wiesel. New York: Schocken Books, 1982.

———. *The Fifth Son*. Translated by Marion Wiesel. New York: Summit Books, 1985.

———. "The Accident," in *The Night Trilogy*. Translated by Anne Borchardt. New York: Hill and Wang, 1990.

———. *Evil and Exile*. Translated by Jon Rothschild. Notre Dame, IN: University of Notre Dame Press, 1990.

———. *From the Kingdom of Memory: Reminiscences*. New York: Summit Books, 1990.

———. *The Forgotten*. Translated by Stephen Becker. New York: Summit Books, 1992.

———. *Somewhere a Master*. Translated by Marion Wiesel. New York: Touchstone, 1993.

———. *All Rivers Run to the Sea*. Translated by Marion Wiesel. New York: Alfred A. Knopf, 1995.

———. *And the Sea Is Never Full: Memoirs, 1969*. Translated by Marion Wiesel. New York: Alfred Knopf, 1995.

———. *The Testament*. Translated by Marion Wiesel. New York: Schocken, 1999.

———. *Night*. Translated by Marion Wiesel. New York: Hill and Wang, 2006.

———. *Open Heart*. Translated by Marion Wiesel. New York: Alfred A. Knopf, 2012.

Wiesel, Elie and Richard D. Heffner. *Conversations With Elie Wiesel*. Edited by Thomas J. Vinciguerra. New York: Schocken Books, 2003.

Wiesel, Elie and Philippe Michael de Saint-Cheron (editors). *Jews of Silence*. Translated by Neal Kozidoy. New York: New American Library, 1966.

ARTICLES

Aarons, Victoria. "'The Past Became the Present,' Reenactment of Trauma in Elie Wiesel's *The Gates of the Forest*," *Literature and Belief*, 26, no. 1, 2006.

Berger, Alan. "Interview of Elie Wiesel," *Literature and Belief*, 26, 2006.

Habertal, Moshe. "The Dance Goes On," *New York Review of Books*, May 2018.

Katz, Steven T. "Elie Wiesel: The Man and His Legacy," *Yad Vashem Studies*, 44, December 2016.

Pawlikowski, John. "Creating an Ethical Context for Globalization: Catholic Perspectives in an Interreligious Context," *Journal of Ecumenical Studies*, 42, no. 3.

Seidman, Naomi. "Elie Wiesel and the Scandal of Jewish Rage," *Jewish Social Studies Series* (Series 2), 3, no. 3, 1996, 8.

Suro, Roberto. "John Paul Holds Waldheim Meeting," *New York Times*, June 26, 1987.

CHAPTERS

Aarons, Victoria. "On the Periphery: The 'Tangled Roots' of Holocaust Remembrance for the Third Generation," in *Third Generation Holocaust Representation: Trauma, History, and Memory*. Victoria Aarons and Alan L. Berger. Evanston, IL: Northwestern University Press, 2017.

Berger, Alan L. "Elie Wiesel," in *Interpreters of Judaism in the Late Twentieth Century*. Edited by Steven T. Katz. Washington, D.C.: B'nai B'rith Books, 1993.

———. "Interview With Elie Wiesel," in *The Continuing Agony: From the Carmelite Convent to the Crosses at Auschwitz*. Edited by Alan L. Berger, Harry J. Cargas, and Susan E. Nowak. Academic Studies in the History of Judaism. Binghamton, NY: Binghamton University Press, 2002.

———. "Elie Wiesel: Writer as Witness to and in Exile," in *Exile in Global Literature and Culture: Homes Found and Lost*. Edited by Asher Z. Milbauer and James M. Sutton. New York: Routledge, 2020, pages 102–116. Camus' influence on Wiesel is ubiquitous. Perhaps nowhere as striking as in Wiesel's statement: "When I look around the world I see nothing but hopelessness. And yet I must, try to find a source for hope. We must believe in human beings in spite of human beings." Robert Francoisi (editor). *Elie Wiesel: Conversations*, page 146.

Clair, Janet. "Common Ground and Holy Ground: Prayers of the Holocaust," in *Remembering for the Future*. London: Palgrave Macmillan, 2001.

Feingold, Henry L. "Did American Jewry Do Enough During the Holocaust?" in *Judaism in the Modern World*. Edited by Alan L. Berger. New York: New York University Press, 1994.

Feinstein, Margaret Myers. "Reconsidering Jewish Rage After the Holocaust," in *The Palgrave Handbook of Holocaust Literature and Culture*. Edited by Victoria Aarons and Phyllis Lassner. Cham, Switzerland: Springer, Palgrave Macmillan, 2020.

Green, Arthur. "Wiesel in the Context of Neo-Hasidism," in *Elie Wiesel: Jewish, Literary, and Moral Perspectives*. Edited by Steven T. Katz and Alan Rosen. Bloomington: Indiana University Press, 2013.

Lamont, Rosette C. "Elie Wiesel: In Search of a Tongue," in *Confronting the Holocaust: The Impact of Elie Wiesel*. Edited by Alvin H. Rosenfeld and Irving Greenberg. Bloomington: Indiana University Press, 1978.

Polen, Nehemia. "Yearning for Sacred Place: Wiesel's Hasidic Tales and Postwar Hasidism," in *Elie Wiesel: Jewish, Literary, and Moral Perspectives*. Edited by Steven T. Katz and Alan Rosen. Bloomington: Indiana University Press, 2013.

Rosen, Alan. "Capturing the Fire, Envisioning the Redemption," in *Elie Wiesel: Teacher, Mentor and Friend*. Edited by Alan L. Berger. Eugene, OR: Cascade Books, 2018.

Roth, John K. "Wiesel's Contribution to a Christian Understanding of Judaism," in *Elie Wiesel: Jewish, Literary, and Moral Perspectives*. Edited by Steven T. Katz and Alan Rosen. Bloomington: Indiana University Press, 2013.

———. "The Impact of Elie Wiesel," in *Elie Wiesel: Teacher, Mentor, and Friend*. Edited by Alan L. Berger. Eugene, OR: Cascade Books, 2018.

———. "Wiesel and Talk About Religion in Public," in *Celebrating Elie Wiesel: Stories, Essay, Reflection*. Edited by Alan Rosen. Notre Dame, IN: University of Notre Dame Press, 1998.

Miscellaneous

Astro, Alan. *PowerPoint*. Dallas, TX: Ackerman Center for Holocaust Studies, 2018.

Eisenhower, Dwight D. *For the Dead and the Living, We Must Bear Witness*. United States Holocaust Memorial Council, postcard.

Jacoby, Jeff. "Elie Wiesel's Love of America," *Boston Globe*, 2016.

Rittner, Carol. "Afterword," in *Elie Wiesel: Teacher, Mentor, and Friend*. Edited by Alan L. Berger. Eugene, OR: Cascade Books, 2018.

Wiesel, Elie. "The America I Love," http://www.thehypertexts.com/Essays%20Articles%20Reviews%20Prose/Elie_Wiesel_The_America_I_Love.htm. Accessed September 10, 2016.

———. "Brooklyn: A New Hasidic Kingdom." Translated by Marion Wiesel. Elie Wiesel Collection, Gottlieb Archive. Boston: Boston University Press, 1975.

———. "Foreword," in *Were We Our Brother's Keepers? The Public Response of American Jews to the Holocaust 1939–1944*. Contributed by Haskel Lookstein. New York: Hartmore House Publishing, 1985.

Wiesel, Elie and Oprah Winfrey. "Auschwitz Death Camp," DVD Harpo Inc., 2005.

———. "We Are All Witnesses: An Interview with Elie Wiesel," *Parabola*, X, no. 2, "Exile," Summer 1975.

INDEX

Printed in the United States
by Baker & Taylor Publisher Services